S0-BIE-599

THE LIBRARY OF GRAPHIC NOVELISTS™

COLLEEN DORAN

AARON ROSENBERG

The Rosen Publishing Group, Inc., New York

To Jeremy—you see, it can happen

Published in 2005 by The Rosen Publishing Group, Inc.
29 East 21st Street, New York, NY 10010

First Edition

Library of Congress Cataloging-in-Publication Data

Rosenberg, Aaron.
Colleen Doran / by Aaron Rosenberg.— 1st ed.
p. cm. — (The library of graphic novelists)
Includes bibliographical references and index.
ISBN 1-4042-0283-8 (library binding)
1. Doran, Colleen, 1963– 2. Novelists, American—20th century—
Biography. 3. Graphic novels—History and criticism.
4. Graphic novels—Authorship.
I. Title. II. Series.
PS3554.O593Z87 2005
741.5'973—dc22

2004011068

Manufactured in Malaysia

CONTENTS

INTRODUCTION

Most people assume that the graphic novel grew out of the comic book. After all, the standard description of a graphic novel is "a long comic book." But that's not quite true. The two forms do share certain traits. Both graphic novels and comic books are stories told through the use of illustrations in sequential form. But because comic books are shorter, their stories tend to be simpler. Graphic novels are longer and often more serious. In a way, it's best to think of comic books as graphic short stories. Most people saw comic books first, so they assume the comic book is the original form. Actually, graphic novels came first.

It is difficult to say which was the first graphic novel, but many historians agree that it was *The Adventures of Obadiah Oldbuck*, written and illustrated by Rodolphe Toffler and published in the United States in 1842. In 1897, a cartoon

Comics aren't just for kids, and they're not limited to stories of superheroes saving the world. Comics stores stock their shelves with a variety of comics and graphic novels, proving there is something for everyone in the genre. Graphic novels have become so popular that mainstream bookstores like Barnes & Noble often give them their own section.

strip called *The Yellow Kid* was collected (meaning the individual cartoon strips were compiled in sequential order and printed several to a page) as a magazine. This was the first graphic collection that made a profit. It was more than thirty years before M. C. Gaines published the first comic book, *Funnies on Parade*, in 1933. Action Comics number 1, which introduced *Superman* to the world, appeared in 1938.

Over the years, new graphic novels appeared, but these were mainly in Europe and Asia. Readers in the United States were more interested in comic books, and particularly in superheroes, which were perfect for kids and cheap enough for them to afford. In the late 1970s, however, comic-book sales were down, and publishers needed new ways to reach their audience. Before this, comic books had been sold at newsstands and in bookstores or grocery stores. Now, comic-book publishers began selling their comics directly to them instead. Because these stores carried only comic books, they were willing to buy a wider variety of comics, unlike the newsstands, which had limited space. This gave comic-book publishers more freedom to experiment, both with content and with form. They could try different types of comic books because they knew most comic-book stores would buy a few to test them out.

In 1978, Marvel Comics released *The Silver Surfer*, a graphic novel about the superhero by that name. This was the first mass-market trade paperback graphic novel—the first book to use the same format as graphic novels today. Eclipse followed with its graphic novel

One of the earliest comic strips to be collected and published in book form was The Yellow Kid. *This issue (volume 1, number 2) was published on April 3, 1897. The creator of* The Yellow Kid, *R. F. Outcault, was a pioneer in the comics industry. His Yellow Kid was a popular comic character—so popular he boosted newspaper sales and was heavily merchandised.*

Sabre, a science-fiction tale whose creators (Don McGregor and Paul Gulacy) retained all rights to the story. Before this, major publishers had bought all rights from the creators, so comic-book writers and artists had little incentive to do their best work. Now, however, writers could work on the books they wanted to do, retain control of the characters, and make more money if the books did well. *Elfquest*, which appeared a year or two later, was the first creator-owned series to appear in regular bookstores as well as in comic-book stores, and this book is still one of the standards for the independent graphic novel.

By the mid-1980s, the form had been established, and writers and artists began to push it. They produced graphic novels in different genres and with different art styles. Some graphic novels featured standard superheroes, but others told more serious stories. One of the most successful graphic novels ever, *Watchmen* by Alan Moore and Dave Gibbons, was a DC Comics miniseries about superheroes told in a more realistic fashion. In 1986 and 1991, a cartoonist named Art Spiegelman released a pair of books called *Maus: A Survivor's Tale*, which told the story of his parents' experiences in World War II concentration camps using mice, cats, and other animals as characters. The book won a Pulitzer Prize in 1992 and proved to the world that graphic novels could have serious content and brilliant writing.

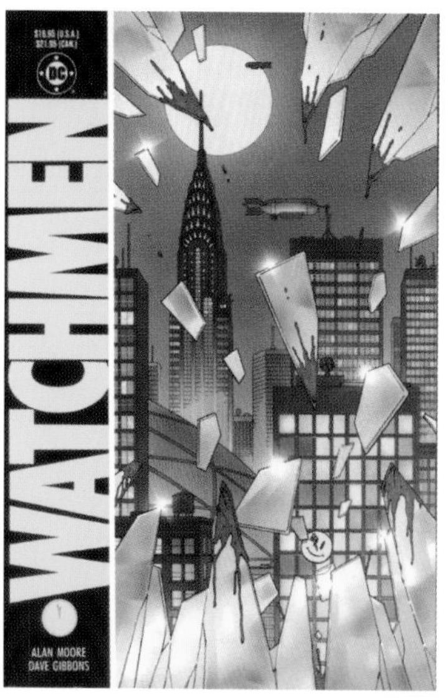

Together, writer Alan Moore and artist Dave Gibbons created the now classic graphic novel *Watchmen*. The story was released as a twelve-issue series beginning in 1986. *Watchmen* offered a unique take on the superhero genre, but more important, it was a groundbreaking work that forever changed the way people thought of graphic novels.

Graphic novels have become as popular as comic books for several reasons. First, some people do not want to wait months for each new issue of a comic to come out. A twelve-issue, monthly comic-book series can take one year (or longer) to collect, even if every issue appears on time. A graphic novel allows the reader to enjoy the entire story at once, just like he or she does when reading a regular novel. A second reason is that graphic novels are becoming easier to find. Comic-book stores are disappearing, and many mainstream bookstores still don't carry comic books, but most have graphic novels in the science-fiction and fantasy section. Some people still mock anyone who reads a comic book because they think comic books are for little kids. But graphic novels, because their thickness and sturdier covers seem closer to those of novels, are considered more adult and more acceptable. Another reason is that more and more comic-book creators are turning to the graphic novel as their medium of choice. Comic books are usually only twenty to thirty pages per issue, which is not enough space to tell a full story—most comic-book issues are merely chapters in the larger tale of the series. But graphic novels are usually sixty-four pages or more, allowing the artist and writer more freedom to tell the full story in a single volume. Graphic novels also have a wide range of styles, genres, and content, so it's easy for the creators to tell the stories they want to tell without restricting them to subjects a publisher thinks can hold people's interest for months on end.

An inherent advantage to the graphic novel compared to a straight prose novel is that it has illustrations.

Novelists have to write stories so that the reader can see the action and the characters in their heads based solely on words. Graphic novelists provide images along with text, so the creators have multiple layers with which to express their stories. The graphic novel's art can set the tone, working with the words to create a more powerful story. Regular novels often do this with their covers, since a good cover can intrigue the reader before he or she even reads the book. Graphic novels do this with every page, using the art itself to convey more of the story than the words could on their own.

This also means that most graphic novels have two storytellers instead of one. They have both a writer and an artist, and the two work closely together. The stories have the potential to be more textured because two people are contributing to them, in two very different ways, and they build upon one another. A good writer can work around bad art, just as a good artist can improve a weak story, but a good writer and a good artist working together can produce work better than either could manage alone.

Of course, some graphic novelists can do both sides of the equation. They can write and draw. This is a rare skill, and most concentrate on one side or the other. But those who can do both can create their own graphic novel and control every aspect of it to produce a more unified work. One of these rare and talented people is a woman named Colleen Doran.

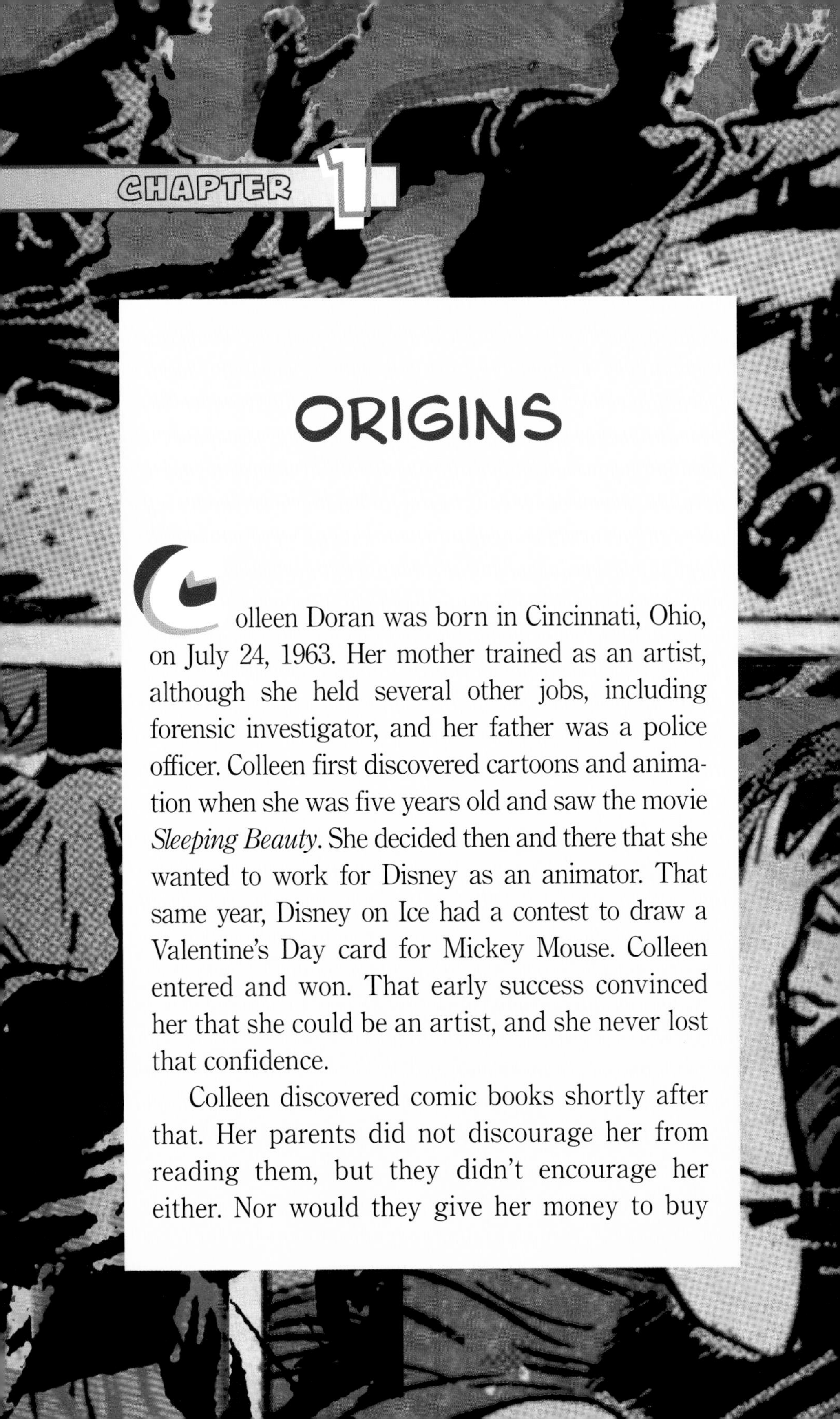

CHAPTER 1

ORIGINS

Colleen Doran was born in Cincinnati, Ohio, on July 24, 1963. Her mother trained as an artist, although she held several other jobs, including forensic investigator, and her father was a police officer. Colleen first discovered cartoons and animation when she was five years old and saw the movie *Sleeping Beauty*. She decided then and there that she wanted to work for Disney as an animator. That same year, Disney on Ice had a contest to draw a Valentine's Day card for Mickey Mouse. Colleen entered and won. That early success convinced her that she could be an artist, and she never lost that confidence.

Colleen discovered comic books shortly after that. Her parents did not discourage her from reading them, but they didn't encourage her either. Nor would they give her money to buy comic books. Colleen solved that problem. She started checking people's trash for soda bottles, which she then redeemed for a nickel apiece. That money was enough to keep her in comic books, and since the money was hers, her parents could not stop her from buying them.

Unfortunately, Colleen's family moved to a more rural area when she was still young. The area did not have a comic-book store, so Colleen could not find many comics to read. She read the *Prince Valiant* comic strip in the newspaper but had very little access to other stories.

When she was twelve, Colleen contracted a severe case of pneumonia. She had to go to the hospital, and even after she was allowed to go home, she remained bedridden for weeks. Forced to miss school, she spent the days drawing to keep herself occupied. While she was stuck at home, a friend of her father's brought her a wonderful present—a box full of comic books. Suddenly, Colleen was able to catch up on years of comics, and she discovered the world of Marvel and DC superheroes.

Even at a very young age, Colleen Doran was a gifted, prize-winning artist. She has been able to combine her artistic talent with her interest in human behavior to create some very interesting comic characters.

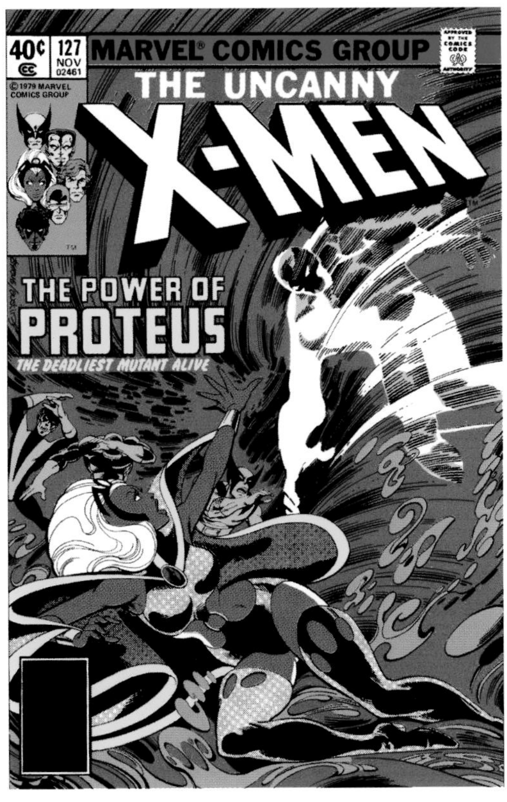

A fan of the popular *X-Men* comics series, Doran drew inspiration from its superheroes. When she first began experimenting with her own drawings, she found herself sketching similar characters. This cover is of *The Uncanny X-Men* number 127, "The Quality of Hatred," published in November 1979. This issue was written by Chris Claremont and John Byrne, penciled by John Byrne, and inked by Terry Austin.

Trying Her Hand at Comics

Although Colleen had soon read through the entire box, the comic books offered her more lasting entertainment. They had shown her a whole new world for artists, and Colleen was hooked. She began inventing her own comic-book ideas, dreaming up characters and stories. She filled sketchbooks with images, often drawing the same character over and over until she was satisfied.

Doran drew this sketch of Jason when she was still in high school. The character is part of her long-running work, *A Distant Soil*. It is interesting to observe Doran's artistic and technical development over the course of her *Distant Soil* issues. This image is published alongside other early Doran sketches in *A Distant Soil* number 34, a 64-page special issue.

At first, these ideas were based on the superhero books she had read, particularly Jack Kirby's *The Eternals*, Nick Cardy's *Teen Titans*, and Chris Claremont and John Byrne's *X-Men*. But after a while, Colleen realized she was less interested in the superhero side. She wanted to know what her characters were like in their real lives, not what they did when they put on a mask and a cape. She wanted to see the depth of the characters, and superhero stories focused more on the persona the heroes had created. So she began stripping away the superhero elements from her own work. But she still

An Interest in Deviant Behavior

When Colleen Doran was young, her family used to discuss police cases over the dinner table. But the part that really fascinated Colleen, even more than the crime scene details, were the minds of the people who could commit such crimes. She found deviant psychology fascinating, and she read every book she could find on the subject. Perhaps this interest in how people think, and in how the mind can take different paths and lead people to believe that certain evils are actually acceptable, is what allows her to draw people whose thoughts and motivations are written on their faces and in their stances. Deviant psychology is about understanding how the mind works and learning to watch for subtle clues that indicate unusual behavior. Training in this subject is invaluable for an artist who tries to create characters filled with such subtleties.

loved fantastical stories and characters, so her work began to focus more on science fiction and fantasy. She soon coalesced everything into a single, epic tale that she worked on whenever she had a spare moment.

But this was not all that Colleen did with her life. When she was a teenager, she worked at an amusement park drawing portraits of visitors. She also enjoyed reading and studying. At one point, she considered becoming a doctor of forensics. Her father, who by then had become a police chief, worked on crime scene investigations, and he would show her and her older brother photos of the scenes. He would explain what the police knew going into the scene, and then Colleen and her brother would examine the photos and try to guess what had happened. He also brought home forensics textbooks, which Colleen spent hours reading. But through all of this, Colleen never lost her interest in art.

Interestingly enough, she never had any formal art training. Her mother gave her some pointers on drawing and painting, and lent her art textbooks to study, but Colleen mostly taught herself. This independence would remain a major hallmark of her professional career. It also helps to explain her versatility. Many artists have only one style, perhaps because they were taught by someone else and absorbed the style of their mentor. Since Colleen had no one to tell her how she should draw, she was free to develop her own styles and experiment with her art. It also explains her willingness to work in multiple genres. Many artists with classical training sneer at science fiction and fantasy. They feel that such genres are not fit subjects for true art. And, of course, comic books are beneath contempt. But Colleen had no such prejudices. She grew up enjoying comic books, and she always remembered her fondness for them and hoped that she could someday give other people the same enjoyment those early artists had given her.

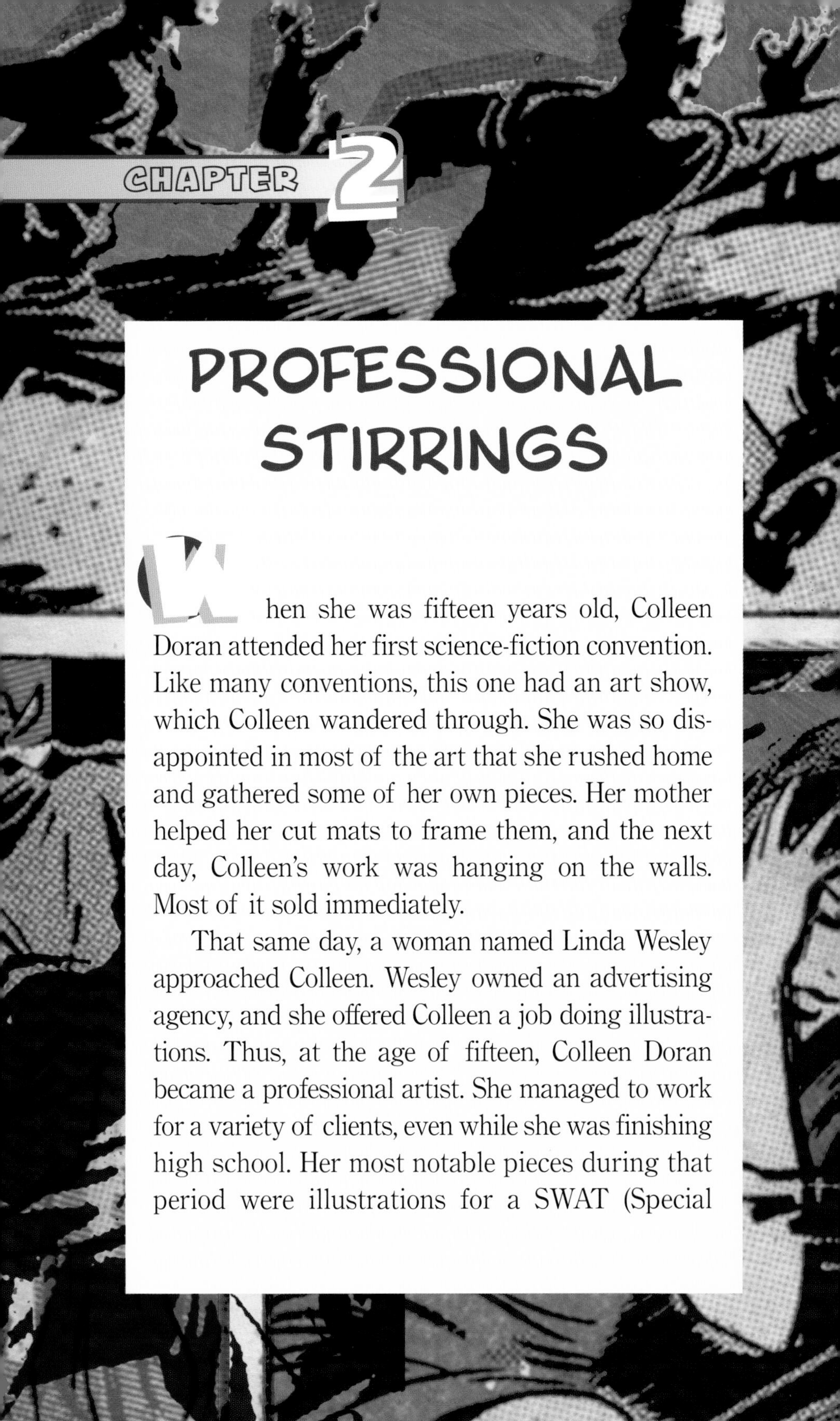

CHAPTER 2

PROFESSIONAL STIRRINGS

When she was fifteen years old, Colleen Doran attended her first science-fiction convention. Like many conventions, this one had an art show, which Colleen wandered through. She was so disappointed in most of the art that she rushed home and gathered some of her own pieces. Her mother helped her cut mats to frame them, and the next day, Colleen's work was hanging on the walls. Most of it sold immediately.

That same day, a woman named Linda Wesley approached Colleen. Wesley owned an advertising agency, and she offered Colleen a job doing illustrations. Thus, at the age of fifteen, Colleen Doran became a professional artist. She managed to work for a variety of clients, even while she was finishing high school. Her most notable pieces during that period were illustrations for a SWAT (Special

Weapons and Tactics) training manual and drawings she did for Planned Parenthood. Sometimes, Colleen worked forty-hour weeks, even while maintaining her class work. Fortunately, her parents supported her career choice and did their best to help her manage her time.

During this time, Colleen also met famed science-fiction illustrator Frank Kelly Freas. He saw her artwork and was impressed enough to talk to her. This began a lifelong friendship, and Freas wrote recommendations for Colleen when she began applying to colleges and for art scholarships.

Unfortunately, balancing college and full-time work proved to be too much. Even though she was allowed to count her professional work toward her art credits, Colleen had so many projects she could not keep up with her other classes. She was forced to leave college early and never went back.

Return to Comics

Colleen had been concentrating on illustrations for ad agencies and other corporate clients, but she had never forgotten her love for comic books. Nor had she ever set aside the epic tale she had created in her teens. Many of her portfolio pieces still centered on that work, and this began to catch the interest of several comic-book publishers.

After that first show, when she was fifteen, one small press offered Colleen a job drawing a female-centered comic book. But after two years, Colleen was forced to leave the project. The story had mutated somehow and had become a very adult story with strong sexual content. Colleen was not interested in working on a project of that sort—especially since she herself was still underage! She canceled the project, returned the publisher's advance, and continued to look for other projects.

During this period, Colleen also struck up a friendship with comic-book writer Keith Giffen. Giffen was writing *Legion of Super-Heroes* at the time, and Colleen was a big fan of the series. Colleen had started participating in an online fan publication for *Legion* and had drawn several illustrations for it. Giffen saw her work online and called her up to see if she would be interested in working on the actual comic book with him. Colleen was thrilled, of course. Unfortunately, she was already so busy doing projects with smaller companies that she could not find the time for such a major book, and she was forced to decline the offer. She and Giffen remained friends, however, and she did eventually work on several *Legion* issues with him.

The Process

Every artist works differently. Some prefer mechanical pencils, others like old-fashioned number two pencils, and still others use sticks of graphite. Then, when they get to the inking stage, some artists go for felt-tip pens, while others turn to quills or rapidographs (a type of technical pen) or even markers. And the choice of paper is equally varied. So what does Colleen Doran use? Pretty much anything.

She does prefer crow quill pens or technical pens for inking, but she has used felt-tips before, particularly when the paper she's working on has the wrong texture for such tools. Her current favorite for painting is oil paint, but she has done covers in the past using watercolors and even pastels. Part of the difficulty in pinning down Doran's choice of tools is that she uses different ones for different effects. If she wants a darker, muddier look, she might go with felt-tips and markers, whereas for cleaner lines, she'll use a crow quill.

Of course, how one works is just as important as what one uses. Artist-writers have an advantage over artists because they don't have to wait for the scripts to arrive. Since they are writing the story and illustrating it, they can simply start drawing whenever they want. And some creators do work that way, sketching the story as it pops into their heads and then cleaning it up later. But Doran has a different approach. She prefers to write out the story beforehand. Once she has the rough draft for the issue, she sketches it onto the pages, determining which scenes go where. Then she pencils the images, adding more detail. After that, she inks the pages, adding the final visual touches, and then she goes back and adds the dialogue. This allows her to modify the dialogue at the end, adjusting it to more closely suit the pictures. At the same time, because she has a draft of the story before she starts drawing the first page, she knows where each issue is going. Artists who make it up as they go often find their stories

Comics artists use a variety of tools in their work. The photograph above shows an assortment of pens, pencils, brushes, and inks. Crow quill pens *(bottom)* are a favorite of inkers everywhere, including Doran. Another favorite, a rapidograph, sits just below the ink bottle.

falling apart partway through an issue, or they just lose interest. But Doran plans hers first, so she knows that when she begins drawing, the story is strong enough to keep readers interested from start to finish. Of course, it takes longer this way than if she finished one portion of the work before doing another, but the result is a more seamless whole. And that helps explain why her work, particularly *A Distant Soil*, so smoothly melds story and art.

Frank Kelly Freas (*inset*) served as Colleen Doran's mentor for many years. Working for Freas exposed Doran to the nuts and bolts of making a living as an artist and is without a doubt a major reason why Doran feels compelled to advise young comics creators on the practical sides of the business. The piece shown above is Freas's 1977 album cover for *Green Hills of Earth*.

Finding a Mentor

Despite steady work, Doran had difficulty making a living as an artist. This was partially because she was not being paid much money for her work. But she also had trouble managing her money and her time. By the time she had turned twenty, she was finally making a living, and that year she moved out of her parents' house. She wound up moving back in soon after, as she discovered that living on her own made matters even more difficult.

It was during this time that Doran and Frank Kelly Freas became much closer friends. His wife had passed away, and Freas was unable to manage his personal affairs and his professional work—just as Doran had had problems living on her own. She wound up becoming his unofficial assistant, and every day she would drive to his house—a three-hour round-trip—to cook and clean and help him manage his business. Though Freas couldn't pay her for her work, he did provide invaluable advice, and he became her mentor. But he didn't teach her how to draw—he felt that she already knew that. Instead, he told her stories about his own life and his experiences as a professional artist. From these stories, and from watching and helping him get his business back in order, Doran learned a great deal about the professional side of the business. She learned how to handle her money and her contracts, and how to manage her time.

A few years later, Doran moved out of her parents' house again. But this time, she stayed out. She bought a

FRANK KELLY FREAS

Born on August 27, 1922, in Hornell, New York, and raised in Canada, Frank Kelly Freas (whose last name is pronounced "FREEZ") is considered one of the most popular science-fiction artists in the world. He has been active in the field since 1950, when he drew the cover for the November issue of *Weird Tales*. He was studying at the Art Institute of Pittsburgh at the time. He won the Hugo Award for Best Professional Artist in 1955 and again in 1956. In 1957, he accepted a job with *Mad* magazine, and after a few interior features, he became its regular cover artist, a position he held until 1962. Freas continued to work in the science-fiction field and continued to win awards. He has been nominated twenty times for the Best Professional Artist Hugo Award and has won ten times. His posters commissioned by the National Aeronautics and Space Administration (NASA) hang in the Smithsonian, and he designed the crew patch for the *Skylab I* astronauts. Freas has also painted women on the noses of World War II bombers, done saints' portraits for Franciscan monks, illustrated record and CD covers, and been commissioned to create biomedical art. In 1971, he published a collection of his black-and-white illustrations from *Astounding* magazine as *The Astounding Fifties*, and in 1977, he wrote his memoir, *Frank Kelly Freas—The Art of Science Fiction*. The sequel, *Frank Kelly Freas—A Separate Star*, came out in 1984. Best known for his sense of humor, his love of the science-fiction genre, and his skill at depicting individuals, Freas is still working today.

home of her own shortly after that and maintained it for many years. Part of her reason for going out on her own was that she was getting more and more assignments and making more money. But it was also because she had learned more about how to handle herself, personally and professionally. Colleen Doran had grown up.

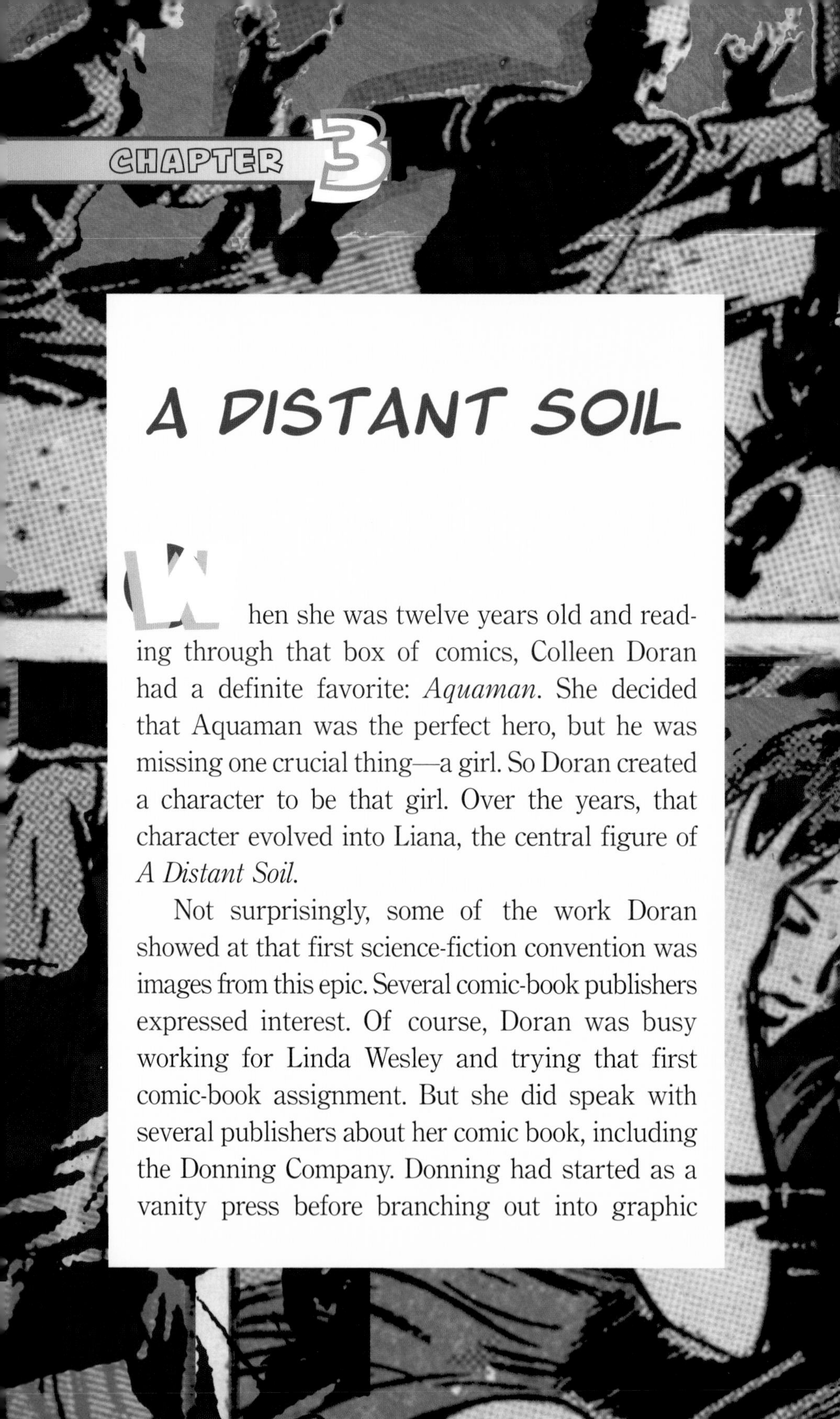

CHAPTER 3

A DISTANT SOIL

When she was twelve years old and reading through that box of comics, Colleen Doran had a definite favorite: *Aquaman*. She decided that Aquaman was the perfect hero, but he was missing one crucial thing—a girl. So Doran created a character to be that girl. Over the years, that character evolved into Liana, the central figure of *A Distant Soil*.

Not surprisingly, some of the work Doran showed at that first science-fiction convention was images from this epic. Several comic-book publishers expressed interest. Of course, Doran was busy working for Linda Wesley and trying that first comic-book assignment. But she did speak with several publishers about her comic book, including the Donning Company. Donning had started as a vanity press before branching out into graphic novels and trade paperbacks. Its representatives liked what they saw of *A Distant Soil*, and they wanted to publish it. But then the publisher found out that Doran was only fifteen and refused to work with someone so young. Fortunately, one of his employees showed Doran's portfolio to another publisher, Warp Graphics. Warp was also interested and was not concerned about her youth. A year later, Warp signed a contract with Doran, and *A Distant Soil* found a home. Unfortunately, Keith Giffen's call asking Doran if she wanted to work on *Legion of Super-Heroes* came right after those contracts had been signed, so Doran had to decline his offer so that she would have time to work on *A Distant Soil*.

A Second Chance

Years later, in 1987, Doran and *A Distant Soil* wound up back at Donning. Donning was actually one of eight companies to bid on the book, alongside Marvel's Epic line, Dave Sim's Aardvark Vanaheim, and the brand-new Dark Horse Comics. But Donning offered Doran something no one else did—a chance to start over. Donning loved the book and knew Doran wasn't happy with what Warp had done to it. So the company offered her the chance to rewrite and redraw the comic from the beginning—in color. The other contenders wanted to continue the story from where Warp had left off, which would have meant that all of its changes would become permanent. Doran didn't want anything from Warp left in her story, so she accepted Donning's offer.

Her relationship with Donning was far more cordial than her relationship with Warp, and Doran was allowed to keep full creative control over the book. The books sold well, too—she released two trade paperbacks, *A Distant Soil: Immigrant Song* and *A Distant Soil: Knights of the Angel*, which sold, between them, roughly 30,000 copies, an unheard-of number back then. Unfortunately, even with those sales, Donning itself was not doing well. The publisher had started as a small press and had never really learned how to handle being more successful. Rather than hiring more staff and reorganizing, it tried to continue as it had been and made a complete mess. Part of the problem was that Donning had never figured out how to handle the direct sales market, so it lost potential sales because of its ignorance. A short time after *Knights of the Angel* came out, Donning sold its trade division to another publisher. It also sold the rights to all its existing titles, but the creators banded together and filed a class-action lawsuit to prevent their work from being sold to a publisher they knew nothing about. The case was settled out of court, and the creators regained control of their titles. That meant that *A Distant Soil* was homeless yet again.

Doran had had enough of getting burned by publishers. She didn't trust anyone else to publish the book the way she wanted it done. She was also getting a lot more comics illustration work, mostly from DC and Marvel, and didn't really have time to court another publisher. But *A Distant Soil* just wouldn't go away.

She had considered self-publishing before. In fact, after signing all the publishing rights over to Donning,

Doran knows that her fans are interested in any extras she can provide them. She is not too proud to show her early work, and she often publishes early sketches and attempts in special issues and in the back of *A Distant Soil* issues. Left: Early sketches of Jason and Liana, which Doran calls "embarrassing," show a prodigious talent. Doran humbly asserts that hard work and practice made up for what she lacked in talent. Right: A page from an early work, *A Distant Soil: Seasons of Spring*, also drawn when Doran was only in high school.

Doran had asked for the black-and-white rights back. That way, if she wanted to, she could have published issues herself in black and white, and then colored them and handed them to Donning for re-release. Now that Donning had given back all the rights, she could do color or black and white herself. But could she really afford it?

No matter how busy she became with other projects, Doran couldn't give up the idea of doing *A Distant Soil* the way she wanted it. Finally, in 1991, she gave in to the inner pressure and decided to self-publish. It wasn't easy. Her company, Aria Press, published its first issue in June 1991. The early issues were reprints of the Donning issues, but

LEGAL DISPUTES

When Donning decided it couldn't work with someone as young as Doran, she took her story to another publisher, Warp Graphics. Warp was enthusiastic about the project, and Doran was thrilled that her baby would finally see print.

In retrospect, it was not the best decision. Warp claimed to love everything about the comic book, but once it was in the editors' hands, they demanded changes, several of which they made on their own. When Doran protested, Warp claimed that it owned the comic book and that Doran had no rights to it. Of course, this was not true at all. The only part of the book Warp did create was the title, *A Distant Soil*, which they took from a poem by Thomas Gray. Doran had originally called the book *The Rebels*.

After nine issues and constant arguing, Doran decided that the arrangement simply wasn't working. She took her book back and walked away—or tried to. Warp refused to give up the rights, and they wound up going to court. Finally, years later, the issue was settled, and Warp acknowledged that *A Distant Soil* was actually Doran's creation. She retained full rights to the comic and even got the right to use that title. The episode left a bitter taste in her mouth, however, and even though it did not dim her enthusiasm for comics, it did make Doran a bit more wary. To this day, she will not discuss the details of what happened. In part this is because Warp, or its former employees, can still sue her if she says anything negative about it. But it is also because she wants to put that whole episode behind her and move on with her life and with her comic book.

done in black and white with some additional pages. Doran had been working in comics for years, but she had never tried publishing before. It was an eye-opener. Printers overcharged her and tried to steal the negatives to her art. Distributors demanded insane discounts. But Doran persevered. She learned how to organize her time more efficiently, how to handle market demands, and how to put her foot down. *A Distant Soil* was soon selling better than ever, and Doran had made a name for herself as one of the strongest of the comic-book self-publishers.

Fortunately, Doran started self-publishing at just the right time. The early 1990s were a growth period for comic books in general and for independents in particular. Readers couldn't get enough of these creative new ideas, and books were selling better than ever. The first issue of *A Distant Soil* sold through four printings, an amazing feat. Doran contracted pneumonia in 1992, as serious a case as she had when she was twelve, and she almost died. But she told herself that she couldn't give in to the illness because her book was doing so well, so she forced herself to get better and to keep writing, drawing, and publishing.

It takes a lot of money to self-publish, which means that it can take a long time before a small company becomes successful. Even with such impressive sales, it took Aria Press until issue 9 before it was actually out of danger and making money steadily. Issue 11 was the last issue to include any of the old Donning material, and with issue 12, Doran began telling a new section of the story.

Unfortunately, in 1995, the comic-book market suffered a major collapse. Marvel Comics decided to bypass the distributors and sell its books directly to retailers.

This is the cover from the first issue of *A Distant Soil* that Colleen Doran self-published under the name Aria Press in June 1991. Doran took a tremendous risk by publishing her work herself, but along with the full control she enjoyed, what she learned about the comics industry was invaluable.

Suddenly, the distributors had lost their single largest client and all the money that it had brought them. More than a dozen distributors collapsed in less than six months. This meant that they couldn't pay what they owed to the publishers whose books they had bought. It also meant that some comic-book stores, faced with losing their distribution system, couldn't survive either. And the publishers found themselves losing money on successful books because the distributors didn't have the money to pay them since that money was needed to produce the next issue.

Aria was hit as hard as the rest. Doran found herself calling clients, who told her they didn't have the money they owed her. She didn't have the money for the next issue and couldn't see how she could possibly get it.

Then she got a phone call. A few years before, a handful of creators had gotten fed up with Marvel's contracts, which took all rights for anything they created, and they walked out. These writers and artists formed their own company, Image, and each produced his or her own creator-owned books. One of the founders was Erik Larsen, who had created the comic-book series *The Savage Dragon.* Larsen knew Doran—in fact, a few years earlier, he had beaten her out for the job as the regular artist on Marvel's *The Amazing Spider-Man.* When he heard about her company's difficulties, he called and offered her the chance to publish *A Distant Soil* through Image.

Doran was thrilled. Image was an up-and-coming company. It was all creator-owned, and she already knew several of the people involved. More important, it meant she could keep publishing *A Distant Soil* her way, but without all the risk she'd had as Aria Press. She accepted the offer the same day, and *A Distant Soil* became part of the Image line with issue 15 in June 1996. It has been there ever since and has remained one of the most popular black-and-white comic books in America. The comic has sold over 500,000 copies and close to 50,000 copies of its collected trade paperbacks. And it remains a fan favorite, with Web sites and chat rooms devoted to it and fans all around the world. Some are newer fans who have found the series since it moved to Image, while others have been following the comic since it was published by Donning, or Aria, or even Warp.

Examining the Soil

But what is the comic book about? According to the official Web site for the comic, *A Distant Soil* tells the story of Jason and Liana, the children of a fugitive named Aeren. Jason, who was seventeen when the series began, is a Disrupter, which means that he has the power to short-circuit energy systems, including both people and machines. But his sister, Liana, who is only fifteen, is even more powerful. She is an Avatar, which means that she can draw upon the life force of everyone from the planet Ovanan (Aeren's birthplace) and wield that collected energy as a weapon. Avatars are the religious leaders and protectors of Ovanan, and only one can exist at any given time, which means that Liana is a threat to the Ovanan government. The government sends a warship, the *Siovansin*, to destroy her, but Rieken, the leader of the resistance, arrives to save her. He and his bodyguard, D'mer, and several others gather to protect Liana and to destroy the Ovanan hierarchy. But Rieken has secrets of his own, which, if exposed, could destroy everything they believe. Other factions also fight for control of the resistance, and Liana's adopted home world, Earth, is caught in the crossfire.

THE MAGNIFICENT SEVEN

When Doran started self-publishing *A Distant Soil* in 1991, most people couldn't imagine doing a comic outside one of the established publishing houses. Only a handful of writer-artists had the vision, the audacity, and the stubbornness to try it on their own—and even fewer had the talent to succeed. Eight talented individuals showed the rest how it was done, however, and they banded together in the early 1990s to form the group that became known as the Magnificent Seven: Jeff Smith (*Bone*), Dave Sim (*Cerebus*), Martin Wagner (*Hepcats*), Larry Marder (*Beanworld*), Steve Bissette (*Tyrant*), James Owen (*Starchild*), Rick Veitch (*Rare Bit Fiends*), and Doran herself. And yes, that's eight people—the exact group shifted from week to week, and no one else seemed to mind that they had one too many for their title. Members would meet to sign autographs together and to go to conventions. Lines stretched out the door, and larger publishers complained about all the attention these independents were getting. But the more large publishers complained, the more fans loved the independents. They were showing the readers, many of whom wanted to create their own books, that they didn't need to work for one of the big publishing houses. They didn't need to be restrained and controlled and could strike out on their own instead.

A Distant Soil is well known for its complex story line, its rich characterization, its passionate romances, and its tendency to deal with real-world issues, including child abuse, which led to Doran winning the Amy Schultz Memorial Award.

Artists and writers often use people they know for inspiration, and Doran is no exception. Many of the characters in *A Distant Soil* are based on friends and family. Liana herself is a reflection of Doran as a

These panels from *A Distant Soil* show Liana and Jason in a dramatic moment. The brother and sister were the original center of the story, escaping from the orphanage where they were being held against their will. Jason and Liana possess important—and possibly clashing—powers.

teenage girl. Rieken is based on an old college boyfriend, but he also represents Doran's diplomatic side. The character Brent draws upon another old boyfriend, and the character Minetti is a collage of the police officers, all friends of her father's, who she knew growing up. Bast is visually based on Doran's mother, though her personality is completely different.

It takes Doran almost two months to create each issue of *A Distant Soil.* She writes the issue, hands it to her editor, lays out the pages and pencils everything in, then goes back and inks her drawings. She also has columns, secondary stories, and other features in the back of each issue. She has admitted in interviews that one of the advantages of working with Image, as opposed to self-publishing, is that it gives her deadlines, which make her get the work done more quickly. When she was handling everything herself, it was easier to run late because no one was standing around waiting for her to finish.

A Distant Soil Fan Club

When Doran began self-publishing *A Distant Soil,* she started getting a lot of fan mail. She tried to answer when she could, but her work kept her busy. Then several women asked her if they could set up a fan club for the comic book. They wanted Doran to endorse it. She liked the idea, and it didn't require any work from her other than keeping them posted on what she was doing with the comic and occasionally sending them small items they could give to the members, so she said yes. And for a little while, that worked fine.

But then things took a strange turn. Two of the women who ran the club gossiped about a third, and some very personal information was shared with far too many people. Feelings got hurt, people started fighting, and Doran even heard people talking about lawsuits. This was the first she'd heard about the problems, and she spoke with one of the women who ran the club to suggest that club policies be changed to prevent this from happening again. The woman was insulted and quit on the spot. She also threatened to disband the club, but Doran talked her out of that by offering to run it herself.

That was also a mistake. She found out, after she'd been handed all the records, that the club not only had no money but was in debt, and that it owed renewal gifts to all its members. It took a year or more to properly restructure the club and to pay everything off, but by July 1994, the fan club was back in the black and everyone was happy—except the former club presidents, who were upset that they were no longer in charge. Most of the fans, however, appreciated Doran stepping in. Her actions, which cost her quite a bit of time and money, also demonstrated how much she cared about her readers and how far she was willing to go to keep them happy.

Financial Woes (Again)

One recent complication for *A Distant Soil* was a matter of finances. Image had been using a bookstore distributor company called LPC. Unfortunately, LPC wound up going bankrupt in the early 2000s. This meant they were

From *A Distant Soil* number 1, these panels show Rieken and D'mer swooping down to save Liana. It is Rieken's mission to save Liana, and D'mer acts as his bodyguard. But since she is confused by her powers and the many beings trying to destroy her, Liana is uncertain whether she can trust Rieken. Note the style Doran uses to introduce the important character of Rieken. As he and D'mer descend, they seem to break through the atmosphere into Liana's world, then float over to save her.

unable to pay Image for the books they had ordered (and in some cases even sold, because the money had to pay off other debts instead). As a result, creators such as Doran did not get paid for their books. To make matters worse, the first two collections of *A Distant Soil* had recently sold out, so Doran had printed new copies of those while also printing the third collection, which meant that she spent a lot of money on printing.

Orders were strong enough that she figured she would get money back by the end of the year, but then LPC went bankrupt and that money disappeared. Image had also advanced her some money to pay for booths at several conventions, and that meant that the books needed to earn even more before she would see any of the money herself. It took another year before Doran finally received a royalty check for those books. This also meant that she needed to concentrate on paying projects in the meantime, so she had less time than usual to devote to new issues of *A Distant Soil.*

Fortunately, once the check from Image arrived, Doran was finally able to give the series some attention again and produce several new issues. This is particularly important because fans can get impatient. Even fans of *A Distant Soil*, who have been reading the series for years, can get irritable when months go by without a new issue, and some may even give up and turn away before that next issue appears. In order to maintain her readers' interest, Doran has to produce at least two or three issues a year, enough to reassure the fans that she is still working on the series and that it will not suddenly fade away and leave them hanging.

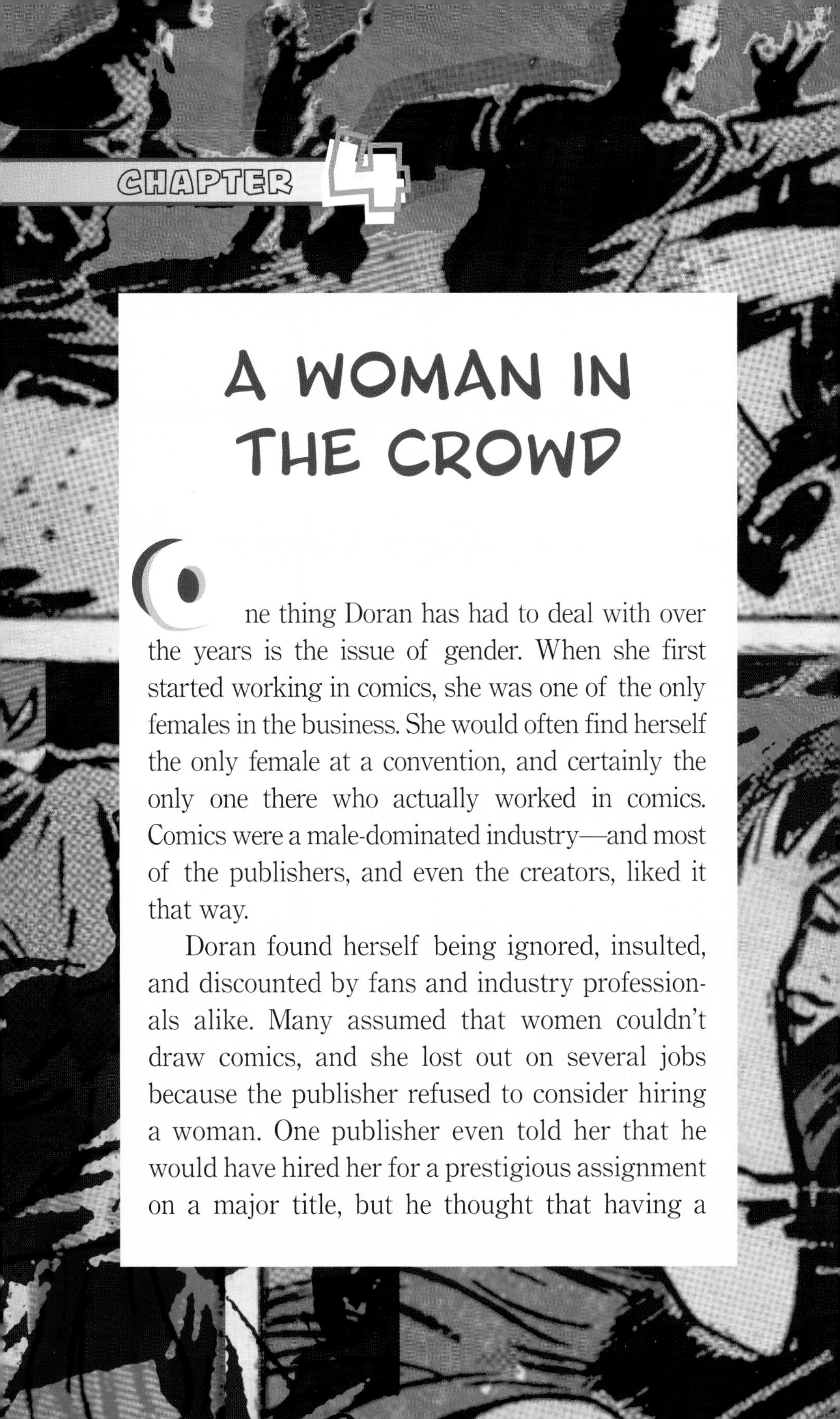

CHAPTER 4

A WOMAN IN THE CROWD

One thing Doran has had to deal with over the years is the issue of gender. When she first started working in comics, she was one of the only females in the business. She would often find herself the only female at a convention, and certainly the only one there who actually worked in comics. Comics were a male-dominated industry—and most of the publishers, and even the creators, liked it that way.

Doran found herself being ignored, insulted, and discounted by fans and industry professionals alike. Many assumed that women couldn't draw comics, and she lost out on several jobs because the publisher refused to consider hiring a woman. One publisher even told her that he would have hired her for a prestigious assignment on a major title, but he thought that having a woman draw a well-known male superhero would scare away the fans. Another editor admitted to her, years later, that he had treated her unfairly and that he had underestimated her talent. But most people never apologized, and the best Doran could hope for was that they would retire and allow younger, more open-minded editors and publishers to take their place.

Several times over the years, interviewers have asked Doran to provide details about some of these incidents. She has always refused. She will sometimes talk about what happened, but she never reveals the names of the people involved and usually restricts herself to stories about people who are no longer in the industry or who have since passed away. Despite what happened to her, she does not consider it appropriate to attack other people or to damage their reputations—even if those people once did the same thing, or worse, to her. But Doran was raised to be polite and gracious.

The treatment she received was no better than the way her work was viewed. Fans either mocked her for being a woman who didn't know anything about comic books (despite the fact that she had been reading them since her early teens) or came on to her because she was one of the only women in sight. And so did the industry professionals. Doran has several stories about editors and art directors who made passes at her, and some who even threatened to withhold her checks if she did not give in to their advances. She refused to be pressured or blackmailed, which led to her being blacklisted

THE BARBIE PROBLEM

One of the dangers in any business is being pigeonholed—having people decide that you can do only one type of work and nothing else. That's particularly dangerous for a creator, because if that happens, he or she may never be allowed to do other kinds of work. And for a woman in a male-dominated industry, the danger is that men may assume that she can do only female-oriented projects.

Doran ran into this situation years back, when she was talking to Marvel about some projects. Marvel wanted her to handle the art on its *Barbie* comic book. Doran knew that if she did, she could get labeled as a "girlie" artist, which would mean that she'd never be allowed to draw anything but cute girls and romance comics. So she told Marvel that she was interested but only if she also got to work on something completely opposite in feel. Marvel finally agreed and let her do a backup feature—a secondary story that appeared in the back of the comic for one or more issues—in its *Hellraiser* comic book. Doran worked on two issues, but her backup stories were so graphic they disturbed people, so Marvel pulled the feature. But the publisher did offer her work on its *Nightbreed* book and stopped asking her to draw Barbie. That was the last time anyone thought she could do only "girlie" pictures.

by certain companies for several years. Some editors never forgave her for snubbing them, and they told everyone that she was talentless and impossible to work with, which cost her even more jobs.

Comic book conventions are the best opportunities for fans to meet their favorite comics creators, get autographs, and get turned on to new comics. Generally, artists and writers like to get feedback and support from their fans. But there are plenty of comic convention attendees who take their interest further than the average fan by dressing up as their favorite characters and bestowing too much attention on the creators. As you can see in this photograph, attendees at these conventions tend to be mostly men.

Doran slowly overcame those falsehoods by demonstrating time and again that she had ample talent and that she could be very easy to work with if the others involved could keep matters on a professional level. Although she had several opportunities to sue people for their discriminating behavior, Doran decided it wasn't worth it. She might have won if she sued, but she would also have earned a reputation as someone who ran to the courts every time someone insulted her. Instead, by handling matters herself and remaining professional no matter what, she gained a reputation for being a strong-willed woman who could handle her own problems and who didn't let a few people's foolish opinions slow her down. Her attitude upset her detractors far more than suing them ever could have done.

Of course, those who liked her could be just as much of a danger. Being one of the few young, attractive women in comics meant that Doran won herself several fans who followed her from convention to convention. Some even called her regularly or sent her mail. Most of these Doran was able to ignore, but one persisted for several years. It was only after a friend of hers called and threatened him, and after she told him she would turn him into the police, that this stalker finally left her alone.

Doran always felt sorry for the few other women she saw in comics because she knew they were dealing with many of the same problems. She has said in interviews that she blames the lack of women in the industry on the comic-book witch hunts of the 1950s,

FRIENDS OF LULU

Friends of Lulu is a national nonprofit organization dedicated to increasing female participation in the comic-book industry. It was founded in 1997 by a group of women led by comics journalist Heidi MacDonald; editor Kim Yale; and author, editor, and publisher Trina Robbins. MacDonald had invited every woman in the industry to a meeting at the San Diego Comic-Con in 1993 to discuss the possibility of starting a professional organization. The organization's name comes from Little Lulu, the assertive comic character created by Marge Henderson Buell.

The organization holds discussions featuring prominent female writers and artists, assembles all-female anthologies, and provides input on what comics might appeal to girls and women and how to reach that audience. It also has recommended reading lists, mailing lists, and a public relations area dedicated to improving the image of comics in general. Both men and women are eligible to join, and the organization welcomes both comics professionals and those who simply enjoy comics and would like to see them reach both genders equally.

Currently, the only active Friends of Lulu chapter is in New York, but it has had chapters in Los Angeles, San Francisco, and Chicago, and is interested in establishing new chapters in other cities as well. Doran works with Friends of Lulu whenever she can because she considers it important to make sure that girls and women are involved in the industry, part of which involves making sure the industry reaches out to them.

In a business dominated by men, it is important for women to have a support network, and the Friends of Lulu is one such organization. The Friends of Lulu Web site is an invaluable resource for women who create comics. The site lists industry events, links to other industry-related Web sites, and business contacts at comics publishers. It hosts message forums and connects fledgling creators with mentors. The site also features a recommended reading list and posts essays from women in the industry.

when comics were accused of being a negative influence on America's youth. Comic-book sales shrank drastically, and many stores stopped carrying them altogether. Only a handful of titles survived, and those were superhero books targeted primarily at boys. That meant girls had no comics to read. They were also actively discouraged from reading comics such as *Superman* and *Batman*, so they found other activities instead. But, since most girls in the 1960s and 1970s never read comics, they never wanted to write or draw them either. This is why Doran was one

Comics artists like Ramona Fradon (*above*) paved the way for Colleen Doran and other female comics creators. Fradon fell into a job at DC Comics in the 1950s, drawing "Aquaman," "Superman," "Batman," and "Plastic Man." She was one of the only women working in comics during that time. Years later, she took over the popular newspaper strip *Brenda Starr*. Instead of seeing herself as a pioneer, Fradon is humble about what she considered to be just a job. "I never enjoyed working on male fantasies—all that hitting and clubbing," she said in an interview that appears on comicspage.com. "That's a man's world and they can have it."

of the few women of her generation to become a comic-book professional.

Now, thanks to her example and the examples of a few others, more and more girls and women are reading comic books again, and more women are drawing them, writing them, and even editing them. Doran still runs into fans who make rude comments about women in comics, but those are few and far between now, and they tend to be laughed out of the room by everyone else. Every time she sees a girl reading a comic book or carrying a portfolio to a convention, she knows that things are getting better.

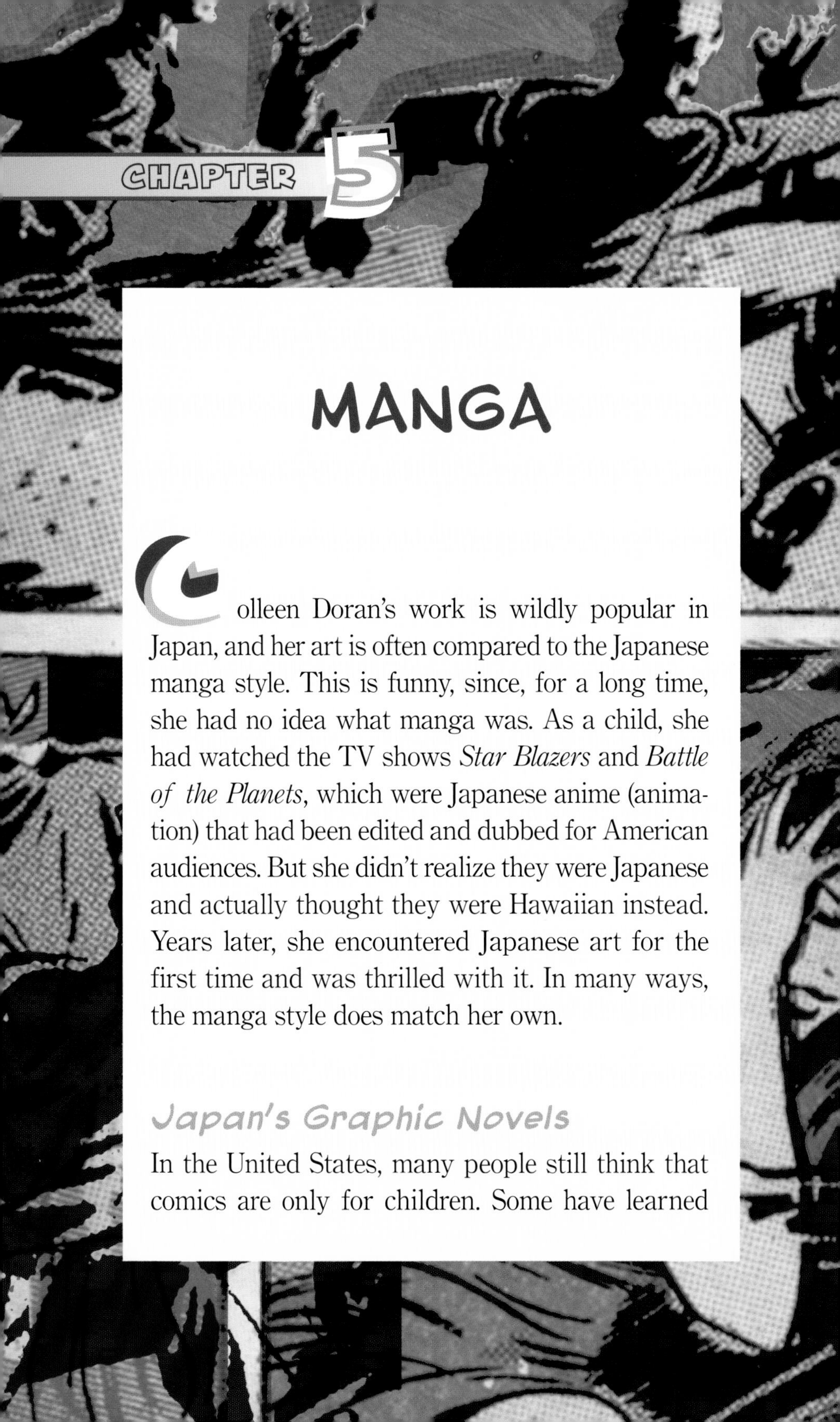

CHAPTER 5

MANGA

Colleen Doran's work is wildly popular in Japan, and her art is often compared to the Japanese manga style. This is funny, since, for a long time, she had no idea what manga was. As a child, she had watched the TV shows *Star Blazers* and *Battle of the Planets*, which were Japanese anime (animation) that had been edited and dubbed for American audiences. But she didn't realize they were Japanese and actually thought they were Hawaiian instead. Years later, she encountered Japanese art for the first time and was thrilled with it. In many ways, the manga style does match her own.

Japan's Graphic Novels

In the United States, many people still think that comics are only for children. Some have learned that comics can have serious stories and high-quality art, but the general image of the comic book is still *Superman* or *Batman*. Japan has a completely different attitude toward comics, however. There, comic books are called manga. These small, thick books are true graphic novels because the stories have all the depth and complexity of a good novel. The only difference is that manga are illustrated. Everyone in Japan reads manga. No one considers it strange to see a grown man reading manga on the subway or two women trading manga books.

Part of the reason manga is so popular there, according to some experts, is the subway itself. Japan has an excellent public transit system, and most people take the train to work each day. Manga are small enough to be carried easily and involved enough to keep a commuter occupied for weeks or even months. American comics, by contrast, are typically too large to carry easily and too flimsy to hold and read one-handed. American graphic novels, too, are too big to fit easily into a coat pocket and too thin to be held easily while one hand is clutching the strap or bar on the train.

The other reason manga is so widely accepted is its style. Manga focuses heavily upon the characters' faces, making it clear that the books are about characterization and drama. American superhero comics focus on the body, particularly the arms and torso, emphasizing action. Most manga are also black and white, which can make them seem much more serious than bright, colorful comics.

Manga is a part of daily life in Japan, and there are few people in the country who do not read it. It is common to see many subway riders reading manga as they travel to their destinations. Manga is printed in a format small enough to be carried around in one's back pocket or bag.

In the past ten years, manga has become a craze in the United States. More and more people in the United States are buying, reading, and trading manga. Comic-book publishers hope this will lead them to American comic books as well, and some publishers have made their own comic books more Japanese in style, even hiring manga artists for the covers. So far, most people have not made the transition. They still see manga and American comic books, even American graphic novels, as two completely separate things. However, the more people enjoy graphic novels, whether American or Japanese, the more people will start to realize that the graphic novel can be used to tell rich and compelling stories.

The History of Manga

Manga has a very long and impressive history. Buddhist monks were creating picture scrolls as early as the sixth century AD. In the 1600s, the Japanese began painting their images onto wood blocks, using a single color and simple outlines and shapes. The artists did not bother to create perfect representations—their images were stylized but easily recognizable.

In 1702, a manga artist named Shumboko Ono assembled a book of his prints, which may have been the first manga in book form. Others refined this technique, creating new and more elaborate books and telling lengthy stories through their images and captions. In 1815, the artist Hokusai invented a new term for this stylized art form. He called it manga, a combination of *man* (which means "lax" or "whimsical") and *ga* (meaning "picture"). The term translates to "a whimsical picture" or "a picture that does not take great pains to copy its subject exactly."

By the end of the nineteenth century, manga-style comic strips had begun to appear in Japanese newspapers. The government censored the comics heavily during the 1920s and 1930s, and shut down many publishing houses. But after World War II (1939–1945), new publishing companies appeared and comics flourished. Most of these comics were produced on very cheap paper and were called *akahon*, or "red books," because of the red ink used on their covers.

One of the red-book artists was a medical student named Tezuka Osamu (1928–1989). Tezuka is considered the father of modern manga. Instead of using the flat imagery that had dominated manga up to that time, Tezuka introduced a more cinematic style, copying the German and French movies he had watched as a student. He drew images at different angles and ranges to create more impact and focused on movements and facial expressions. He would often take pages to show a single motion or emotional display, taking the space to let the images build for greater dramatic impact. As a result, many of his works were a thousand pages or longer.

Tezuka's first comic book, *New Treasure Island,* appeared in 1947 and sold almost half a million copies. Suddenly everyone was buying and reading manga.

Unlike American comics, which were originally intended for children, Japanese manga are for kids and adults—in some ways closer in spirit to the graphic novel. Compare this manga art, from the book *Inu-Yasha: A Feudal Fairy Tale*, by Rumino Takahashi, with Colleen Doran's work in *A Distant Soil*. Note how the art in both cases flows across a page.

Since Tezuka and his successors were creating complex stories with engaging characters and real emotions, no one thought of their work as childish. Their fans continued to read manga as they grew older, and the industry grew with each new generation of readers.

Today, Japan has more than a dozen weekly manga magazines, almost as many biweeklies, and close to two dozen monthlies. Average sales are close to 1 million copies per issue. The paperback sales are almost as high, and manga also forms the basis for Japanese anime. Most American comic-book artists and writers admit they are jealous of manga's success, both how well it sells and how much it is respected. In the United States, most people still consider comic books and graphic novels as something for children, barely a step above children's picture books, and people in the industry are laughed at by "serious artists." But in Japan, manga is widely accepted, and manga artists are treated as the serious and talented artists they are and admired for their skills and the work they produce.

Doran's Relationship with Manga

One major element to Japanese manga art is its attention to detail, and many have noticed the same focus in Doran's work. She admits that she is obsessed with details and loves to fill in every corner of every panel. But the Japanese also use symbolism, drawing particular flowers or shapes that mean a specific emotion or action. Doran has been using symbolism in her art for years, even though, early on, the editors never understood what she was doing with these flowers, shapes, and other background images.

Some Americans have problems with manga because the stories are so drawn out—the first issue or two usually set up the characters and nothing substantial happens, and that is something Doran partially agrees with. She doesn't like the fact that the stories in much of manga take so long to get anywhere, and she definitely prefers to have more action. At the same time, she has been working on *A Distant Soil* since she was twelve, and even the most recent version has been running since 1995, so she's no stranger to taking her time with a story. For Doran, though, there is a difference between a long-term story and a slow story. A story can have such a grand arc that it takes years to tell fully, yet it has so much action that it never seems slow. That is how Doran handles *A Distant Soil*, and it is part of why Japanese readers like her comic so much, because she merges Japanese and American pacing into a style all her own.

One of the most popular manga styles is *shojo*, or girls' comics. Shojo has many romantic elements, but it can include action and even horror. The real key to shojo is its emotional intensity, which fans also appreciate in *A Distant Soil*. Shojo also has a very striking style and relies upon set character types so that readers can instantly tell how a new character fits in the story. Doran doesn't agree with using such stereotypes, but she does have her own clear style for *A Distant Soil*, and its lines and decorative motifs are very shojo.

MANGA STYLES

Manga can be divided into several categories based upon the age and gender of the intended audience. Some manga is aimed at children or teens, while other works are targeted at adults instead. In terms of gender, two clear categories have developed: *shojo* and *shonen*.

Shojo is "girls' comics," manga targeted at women and particularly at teenage girls. These stories are written and drawn almost entirely by women and focus upon girls who find love, win sudden fame, or both. Shojo most often tells love stories and wanders from moment to moment and scene to scene in no clear order. It focuses on the back story, particularly character histories and relationships.

Shonen, or "boys' comics," is completely different. Its stories are more linear, proceeding from start to finish, and usually involve *mecha* (giant robots operated by soldier/pilots who sit in special compartments inside the mecha's head or torso) or supernatural creatures. Shonen concentrates less on relationships and more on action and combat, much the way superhero comics or action movies do in America. It emphasizes plot rather than background details, so shonen stories move more quickly but are less involved.

Of course, some girls read shonen, and some boys read shojo, but most content themselves with the manga aimed at their own gender and with those works that have elements of both but are not restricted to either category. This third type is becoming far more common, and new manga often have both shojo and shonen elements.

Manga has a much larger female audience than American comics in general, which also impressed Doran, particularly since many manga titles were read by men and women alike, rather than being labeled as "women's comics" or "men's comics." *A Distant Soil* has more female fans than male ones, perhaps because it focuses so heavily upon the characters' relationships and emotions, but in Japan, men openly read manga with similar elements.

Since she discovered Japanese art, Doran has become a big fan of both anime and manga. She reads manga whenever she can and also watches anime frequently. Perhaps because her work is so similar to Japanese art, she finds both manga and anime very easy to understand and she loves the lush details.

Another detail Doran appreciates is the Japanese willingness to handle serious topics and real-world issues. *A Distant Soil* touches on several topics that many claim should not appear in comic books, but Doran disagrees. Works such as Art Spiegelman's *Maus* show that some comic-book readers welcome the heavier topics, at least if they are done well. At the same time, Doran merges those topics with romance, fantasy, and action so that her comics provide something for everyone.

In 1996, Doran was invited to attend a comics/manga seminar in Tokyo, Japan, as a guest of Tezuka Productions. She went with Jeff Smith (creator of the comic book *Bone*), Jules Feiffer (Pulitzer Prize–winning cartoonist), Nicole Hollander (strip cartoonist), and

Manga Mania: How to Draw Japanese Comics was written by well-known cartoonist Christopher Hart and published by Watson-Guptill in 2001. A step-by-step guide to drawing in the different styles of Japanese manga, *Manga Mania* features illustrations by Colleen Doran.

Denys Cowan (animator and cartoonist). Doran was delighted to learn more about manga and anime, and was able to compare techniques firsthand with some of the genre's artists. She was also able to meet with several of her Japanese fans, which gave her a new appreciation for Japan's enthusiasm for her work. She has also been invited to Kyoto University in Japan to speak about American comics and how they compare to Japanese manga.

More recently, Doran provided illustrations for two books written by Christopher Hart. The first, *Manga Mania: How to Draw Japanese Comics*, is a how-to book that also discusses the manga industry and the distinctive styles in those comics. Throughout the book, Hart and his collaborators provide examples of the manga art style and step-by-step illustrations of how to draw the standard characters. Doran was one of nine artists to provide illustrations for the book, in part because her own interests matched the manga style so closely.

The second, *Anime Mania*, is about how to draw and create Japanese anime. Of course, manga and anime share some features, but they do require different techniques, just as animated cartoons and comic books do. *Anime Mania* shows not only how to draw anime but how to handle camera angles and special effects, particularly movement. As with *Manga Mania*, this book has step-by-step illustrations to show the reader what to do. Doran did many of the illustrations for the book, and her experience dealing with animated story treatments helped her bring the illustrations to life.

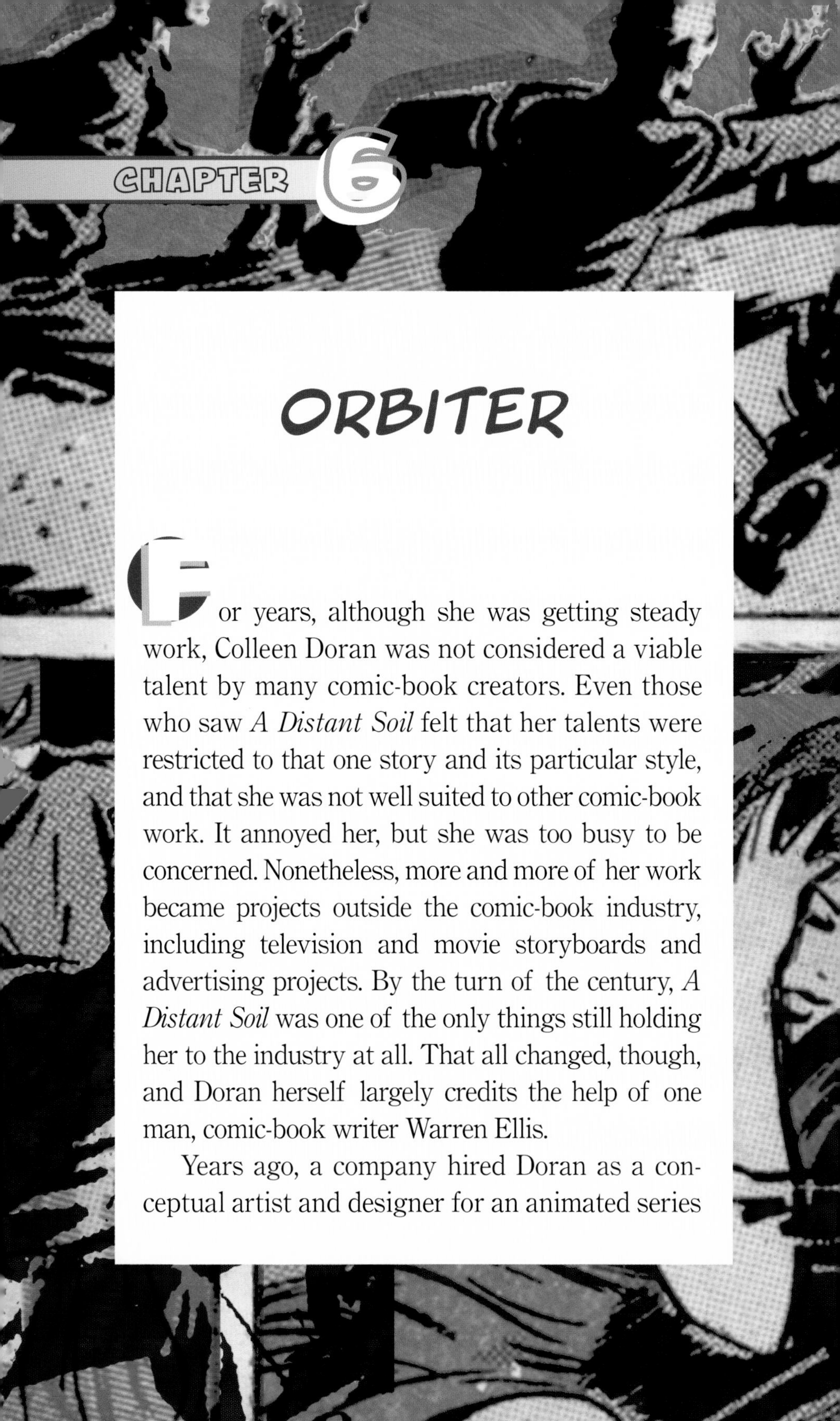

CHAPTER 6

ORBITER

For years, although she was getting steady work, Colleen Doran was not considered a viable talent by many comic-book creators. Even those who saw *A Distant Soil* felt that her talents were restricted to that one story and its particular style, and that she was not well suited to other comic-book work. It annoyed her, but she was too busy to be concerned. Nonetheless, more and more of her work became projects outside the comic-book industry, including television and movie storyboards and advertising projects. By the turn of the century, *A Distant Soil* was one of the only things still holding her to the industry at all. That all changed, though, and Doran herself largely credits the help of one man, comic-book writer Warren Ellis.

Years ago, a company hired Doran as a conceptual artist and designer for an animated series called *Distance*. It hired Ellis to write the series, and Ellis and Doran discovered that they worked well together. *Distance* was optioned by Sony but never wound up being developed. Ellis was impressed enough by Doran's work that in 2001, he asked her to work with him on *Super Idol*, an online Web strip he was producing for ArtBomb.net. That project also went well, so a year or two later, he asked her to handle the art for his next project, a massive graphic novel about a space shuttle and about the future of the U.S. space program. The book's title was *Orbiter*.

Doran was a little skeptical, but not because she couldn't handle the project. She was simply concerned about working with an inker. Her pencil drawings are incredibly detailed, and several times she had been paired with an inker who could not handle such elaborate pages. When that happened, the inker concentrated on the larger elements and ignored all the fine details, which left Doran's work looking stiff, blocky, and amateurish. Part of the reason she hadn't minded not getting as much comic-book work was because she had gotten sick of seeing her art mistreated in that way. But Ellis assured her that it wouldn't be a problem on *Orbiter*. He convinced DC Comics to let Doran not only draw but also ink the book, which meant that every page would look the way she wanted it. Not only did that reassure her, but when *Orbiter* came out, it let everyone see just what her work could look like when it was treated properly.

Award-winning writer Warren Ellis, shown here promoting his book *Transmetropolitan*, wrote the text that accompanied Colleen Doran's artwork in *Orbiter*. Ellis is a prolific and varied writer. In addition to the five years of work on the *Transmetropolitan* series, he has over thirty-five books in print and has also written screenplays and video games.

Pencils and Inks

Most people never realize that comic-book art has two different levels and sometimes even three. Some comic-book artists simply illustrate a book, drawing or painting the pictures. But most books still have two different art credits: penciler and inker. What's the difference?

The penciler does the initial drawings. He or she sketches out all the pages and maps out each scene. Pencilers create the basic images, from the main characters to their equipment to the people standing outside.

But pencilers work in light pencils, and their lines are quick and sketchy. After they've finished setting the scene, the inkers finish the job. An inker does not draw a new image. He or she goes over the pencil lines, giving them solidity. The inker handles the shading, giving depth to the picture, and erases the pencil lines afterward, so that what was a sketchy image becomes a clean one.

Both jobs are important. Without pencilers, inkers would have nothing to finish. But without inkers, pencilers would be left with faintly drawn images. A bad inker can destroy a penciler's work by overdoing the ink lines, ignoring important details, or creating a different mood by using shading and other tricks. But a good inker makes any penciler's art better, giving it more substance, grace, and emotion without losing any of its detail. In the same way, a bad penciler gives an inker nothing to work with. Even the best inker in the world cannot fix a drawing in which the character's arms bend the wrong way or his head looks misshapen. But a good penciler gives the inker a solid foundation, and the inker can concentrate on just cleaning the rough edges and highlighting the important details.

Color comic books have a third artist, the colorist. The colorist gets the art after the inker is done and fills in all the color to the scene. He or she works with the inker's shadings so that a wall with shadows on it might become a blue wall but would still have its shadow. Colorists can also affect the mood of a book; their choices can muddy an image or let the details shine through. Some comic books use digital coloring now, instead of the traditional ink or paint methods.

Sometimes an inker will do the colors as well. Other times, of course, the artist will simply paint or draw the images personally, and no one else will be necessary. Most comic-book artists, though, have had to work with pencilers, inkers, and colorists on books. Knowing how to work together is an important part of the business.

The Orbiter Story

It took Doran two months to research images for *Orbiter* and another fourteen months to draw it. Every page is filled with detail and the art is very distinctive—and completely different from that of *A Distant Soil* or any of Doran's previous work. Some people even claimed that someone else must have done the art, since it did not match her regular style, but Ellis laughed at the idea, and gradually people realized the truth. It wasn't that *Orbiter* was not in Doran's style but that most people had never realized how many styles she could do well. Finally, they were beginning to understand just how versatile she really is.

Orbiter is a 104-page graphic novel about a particular space-shuttle mission. The space shuttle *Venture* was sent out on what should have been a routine mission,

The cover of *Orbiter* shows that Doran is capable of many different art styles. Those used to the style she uses in *A Different Soil* may be surprised to see her work here. Doran has chosen a realistic approach to reflect the grave and sophisticated content of the book. The work shows how Doran has matured and grown, as well as her range as an artist.

going only a few dozen miles outside Earth's atmosphere. But then, shortly into its flight, the shuttle vanished without a trace. The world was horrified and terrified. The government cut back the space program, first restricting missions to robots and sensors and then shutting everything down. Kennedy Space Center was closed down and left to rot, and people drifted onto its grounds and established shelters and crude homes there. No one looked to the stars anymore. Then, ten years after it disappeared, a ball of fire descends upon Kennedy, and within it is the *Venture*. The shuttle makes a perfect landing. It should not be there, should not still be intact, and should not have been able to make the landing it did. Yet there it sits, looking far better than anyone could have expected. And no one knows how it disappeared, where it went, or how it returned. An assortment of scientists and psychiatrists, some of them former members of the space program and others who were born too late to participate, are assembled by the military and escorted to the site. Their instructions are to break into three smaller teams and find out what happened, both by examining the shuttle itself and by speaking to its only remaining occupant, the shuttle's original pilot. No signs are found of the other six crew members, and the pilot has not spoken since his return. Slowly, the three teams piece together the puzzle of the *Venture*'s disappearance and its journeys in the decade since. In the process, they examine the fate of the space program and what its loss means to the world at large.

Doran deliberately chose a different style for *Orbiter*. She went with a heavier line and more muted colors to convey the sense of lost hope that the *Venture*'s disappearance had created. She used a lot of black, often in large blocks of shadow, but none of it was solid. Instead, she crosshatched the blacks (a technique that involves drawing lines at right angles to one another, to create a tiny grid of lines) so that every shadow had more depth and texture.

WARREN ELLIS

Warren Ellis is considered by many to be one of the finest comics writers in the industry today. His work ranges from the science-fiction political satire *Transmetropolitan* to the classic superhero books like *X-Men* and *Batman* to books such as *Planetary* and *The Authority*, which helped redefine the genre. Ellis has demonstrated an ability to tell complex stories and create mysterious but likable characters. He has a knack for believable if vulgar dialogue that breathes an air of believability and depth into his work. He has also written computer games, animated series screenplays, prose fiction, and collections of short stories and journalism. Ellis lives in southeast England with his partner and their daughter.

This full-page panel from *Orbiter* is presented early in the book, when the shuttle is first recovered and the teams of scientists first assembled. Note the detail in Doran's art and the vast amount of research needed to draw such a technical image.

Because the book involved advanced technology, she made sure her drawings were highly detailed, and those involving the shuttle and other instruments had crisp, clean lines that suggested science and order. The backgrounds are filled with small details, and even flat walls have some variety to them, so that every inch of every panel feels alive. Even the cover was a new challenge for her. She printed out a medieval map of the stars on her computer, then tore the map into pieces and pasted it on top of the drawing to create a unique collage of modern and ancient, science and astronomy, all centered upon the stars.

In a bizarre coincidence, *Orbiter* was finished at the end of January 2003, the very week that the space shuttle *Columbia* suffered its own disaster. (On January 16, 2003, the *Columbia* STS-107 lifted off for a seventeen-day science mission. On February 1, 2003, while re-entering the atmosphere, the shuttle suffered a catastrophic failure. All seven astronauts were killed.) Both Doran and Ellis were devastated by the news but decided that the book was now more important than ever. Rather than cancel it, they dedicated the graphic novel to the *Columbia* and its crew. *Orbiter* was released in June 2003 and became DC/Vertigo's best-selling graphic novel in years. It also received excellent reviews, not only in comic book–based publications but also in such magazines as the *Library Journal* and *Bookpage*. Suddenly, Colleen Doran was one of the hottest artists in the industry.

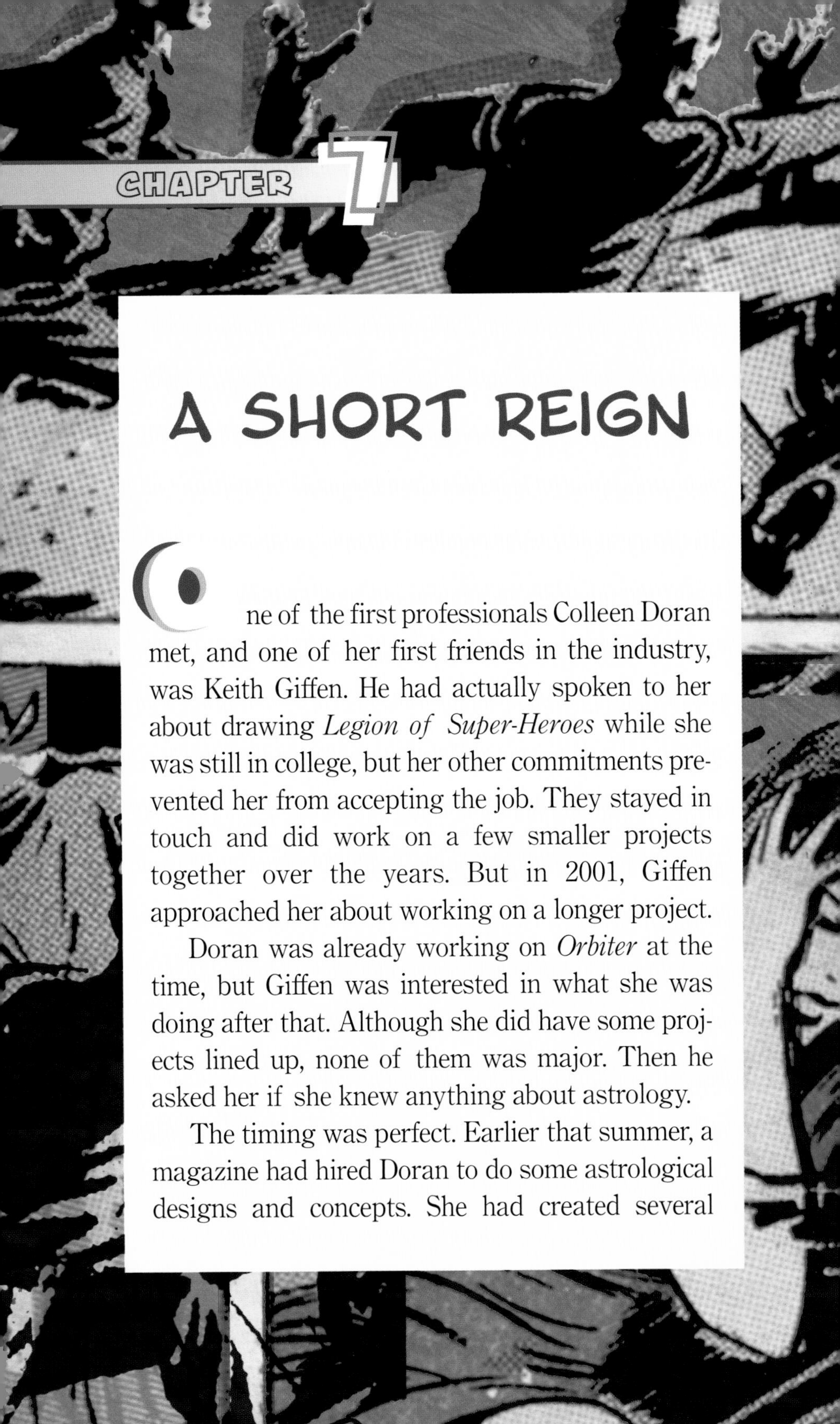

CHAPTER 7

A SHORT REIGN

One of the first professionals Colleen Doran met, and one of her first friends in the industry, was Keith Giffen. He had actually spoken to her about drawing *Legion of Super-Heroes* while she was still in college, but her other commitments prevented her from accepting the job. They stayed in touch and did work on a few smaller projects together over the years. But in 2001, Giffen approached her about working on a longer project.

Doran was already working on *Orbiter* at the time, but Giffen was interested in what she was doing after that. Although she did have some projects lined up, none of them was major. Then he asked her if she knew anything about astrology.

The timing was perfect. Earlier that summer, a magazine had hired Doran to do some astrological designs and concepts. She had created several sketches, which the client had loved, but then it turned out that they were looking for someone who could do computer-based artwork. Doran had never done computer art, so the company hired someone else. But she still had all of the sketches she had done, and her head was still filled with all the astrological details she had learned while researching the project. She showed Giffen the sketches, and he loved them. The two of them pitched the project to DC, and it was approved almost immediately. Doran was still finishing up her work on *Orbiter*, but she and Giffen went ahead and started working on the new project, which was called *Reign of the Zodiac*.

Building the Houses

Part of the challenge, at least for Doran, was finding the right visual style—or styles. She decided that what the book really needed was a different visual style for each of the twelve zodiac houses. That way, when a reader saw a new character, they would be able to tell to which house he or she belonged, just from the art. But that meant Doran had to find a way to visually distinguish each of the houses, and she had to keep the styles close enough that the comic didn't wind up looking like a patchwork quilt.

Costumes were a major element, but that was part of why Giffen had wanted Doran for the job. He already knew that she was a clothing fiend and loved to draw different outfits and different clothing styles. For

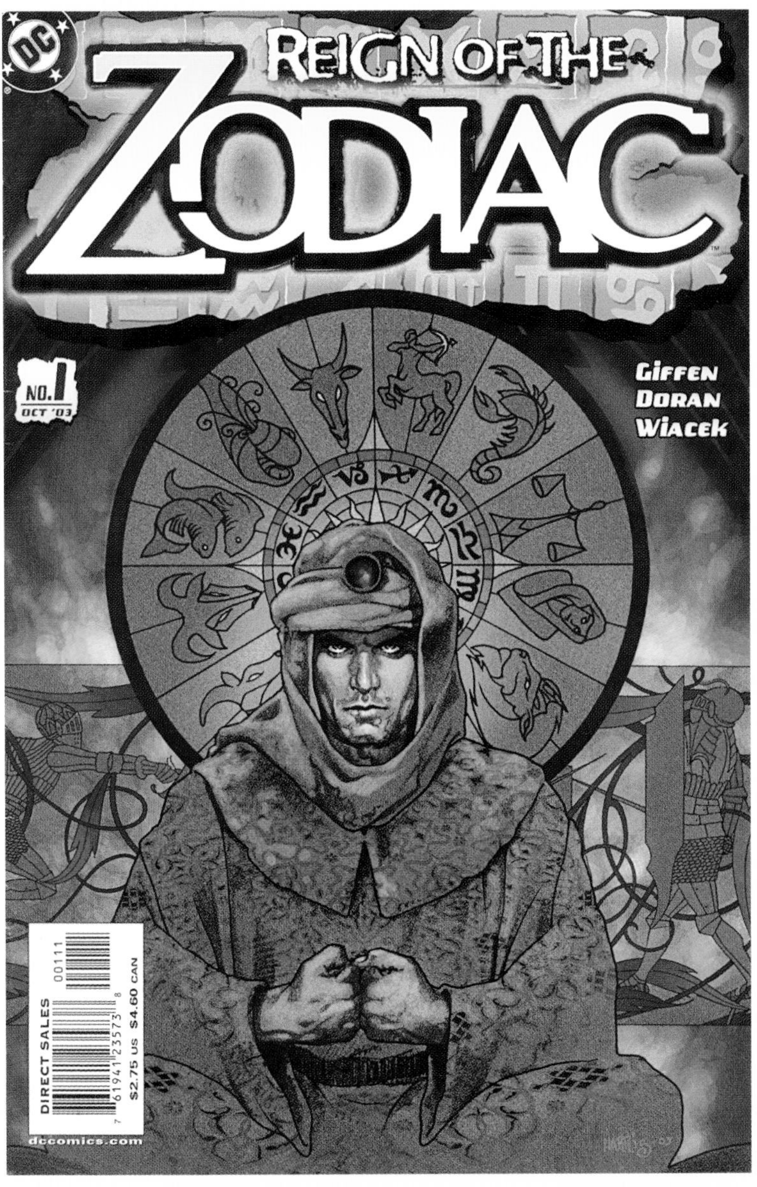

Reign of the Zodiac (the cover of number 1 appears above) was a high-concept project that never quite fulfilled its promise. Doran worked on the project with her longtime friend and colleague Keith Giffen. Even though Doran was sorry the project was cut short, she was grateful for all she learned and produced. She was able to see a bright side when she talked to www.comicon.com: "Most of the work I did never appeared in the book and hasn't been bought, so it belongs to me. I am going to save them for other projects."

Reign of the Zodiac, Doran created over 200 different costume designs.

Fortunately, Giffen allowed Doran a lot of freedom with the art. She actually drew the third issue before starting on the first one, but she wound up changing the style with the first issue and liked it so much that she scrapped what she had already done on issue 3 and drew it all over again. Giffen trusted her and didn't complain. He knew that if he let her have her way, he would get her best work.

Reign of the Zodiac finally hit the stands in July 2003. It told the story of another world, one dominated by the twelve royal houses of the zodiac. The comic book followed the intrigues between the houses and centered upon an arranged marriage that was meant to unite two warring houses—and wound up tearing the world apart instead.

Both Doran and Giffen worked to make the houses distinct. Pisces had elements of czarist Russia, while Scorpio was heavily pre-Columbian. Some of the houses, like Gemini, were more technologically oriented, while Cancer had almost contemporary fashion and sensibilities. Sagittarius drew upon images of old Mongolia. One of the only cultures they did not tap into was Japan, because so many other comics were using that style and culture as a reference point. Doran and Giffen wanted this book to be unique.

For Doran, the book was a wonderful challenge. Not only did she have twelve different houses to draw, each with its own style, but she created incredibly busy,

From *Reign of the Zodiac* number 8, "End of the Worlds," this panel is a good example of Doran's attention to detail and the extraordinary care she took to create a new look for each issue, particularly regarding costumes. Note the ornate, exotic attire worn by the characters in this panel.

detailed pages. The world of the zodiac is filled with people, and every scene has throngs. For an artist like Doran, who is known for her detailed work, such a comic was both a blessing and a curse. It was exciting to get to draw crowd scenes with so many exciting styles, but it also meant that every issue took a long time to produce

KEITH GIFFEN

Keith Giffen was born in Queens, New York, on November 30, 1952. His first publication was a backup feature in Marvel's *Marvel Preview* magazine, which earned him a job as penciler on Marvel's *Defenders* series. He then moved over to DC Comics and worked on various titles. Giffen dropped out of the industry for two years, then came back to DC and eventually wound up as the regular artist on *The Legion of Super-Heroes.* After a brief time away, Giffen went back to the title and remained with the series for thirty-eight issues, writing what many fans call the most controversial story of that comic's long history. Since then, Giffen has worked on various other titles, and at one time wrote for both the *Spider-Man Unlimited* and *Batman Beyond* cartoons. Some comic-book fans hate Giffen, saying he ruined many of their favorite series. Others love him and point out that he rescued many series from oblivion—or that he at least finished them off in style.

because Doran had to detail every single scene on every single page. Plus, she had to work with an inker.

Doran had had mixed luck with inkers. Some of them butchered her work, but this time she got lucky. She wound up with Bob Wiacek. They had worked together before, and she knew that Wiacek respected her enough not to destroy her pencil work. An inker would often get so sick of all the tiny details that he or she would obliterate them with heavy ink lines—or he or she just didn't have enough skill to portray such fine details him- or herself. But Doran knew that Wiacek could handle her pencils and properly ink them. Plus, Doran got the editor to let her do some of the inks herself. That meant that if she drew a page in ink from the start, the editor could just go ahead and use it, rather than make her go back and redraw it. This was particularly easy on those pages that had little or no dialogue because Doran didn't have to worry about where the word balloons would go.

Of course, she and Giffen also had a good working relationship. Most of the story was his, but the two of them talked over each issue beforehand, and he was always willing to listen to Doran's suggestions. In several cases, he changed the story based on something she had suggested. But he had most of the story already worked out, and it was a grand tale. He had conceived the book as being a collection of twelve separate stories, each one six issues long. Each story focused on a different royal house. The entire comic, then, was slated to run seventy-two issues and last six full years.

The Reign Falls

Unfortunately, that did not happen.

Sales on the first few issues were decent but not phenomenal. And the next few issues had lower numbers yet. DC had a meeting to discuss the matter—a meeting that Giffen, Wiacek, and Doran were not invited to attend. At the meeting, the DC editors decided that *Reign of the Zodiac* just wasn't going to make enough money for them to continue publishing it. They announced that issue 8 would be the comic book's final issue.

Naturally, Doran, Giffen, and Wiacek were disappointed. They had had great plans for the book, and now it was over before it had really had a chance to begin. The first story had been about House Aries, and issue 8 had been intended to be the first issue of House Scorpio's story. Giffen had already written it—he had the twelve-issue scripts finished for the entire first year. But now he had to go back and change that issue so that it would serve as a fast wrap-up to the series. And all the other houses would never have their stories told.

Some people blamed the creators for the book's sudden cancellation. A few accused Giffen of thinking too big and of not providing enough in the first few issues to keep readers interested. Others mistakenly claimed that he had announced somewhere that issue 8 was the end of the first story, and that this gave DC an easy way out by cutting the comic off at that issue. Still others said that he simply hadn't made a story that readers could understand and appreciate.

Doran did not escape criticism. A different artist drew issue 7, and several people claimed that the reason was that Doran could not get the issue done on

In this page from *Reign of the Zodiac* number 1, Doran creates a fantastic and overwhelming force that swirls into the twin worlds and wreaks destruction. Since number 1 is the issue that sets the story and introduces the concept of the series, it is important that Doran's artwork attract the reader. This is particularly necessary in the above sequence, which shows the event that precipitates the story: the force that breaks up twelve peacefully coexistent dominions into the twelve houses of the zodiac, set against one another.

time, so someone else had to finish it. They also argued that the delay had thrown off the momentum of the book, and that having someone else draw even a single issue had confused the readers and made them lose faith in the story. In fact, issue 7 had never been assigned to Doran. When DC bought *Reign of the Zodiac*, it had hired her to draw eight issues a year. But then she and Giffen decided to include short story sequences between the major arcs, so they slightly changed Doran's assignment. She was now responsible for ten to eleven issues each year, and the intervening issues would be drawn by someone else. Issue 7 was one of those smaller stories, and it was actually completed before she had even finished the first issue. If the series had continued, someone else would have drawn each of those intervening issues. Of course, some fans might have seen someone else's name on issue 7 and thought that Doran had abandoned the book or failed to get the issue in on time. But they would have been wrong.

Publishing Labels

One of the reasons *Reign of the Zodiac* got canceled was because the sales numbers on its later issues were not very high. And part of that might have been the label. *Reign* was published as a standard DC book. It was not a Vertigo title.

Over the years, DC and Marvel had become associated with superhero comics. Those were, after all, their biggest sellers. Every time they tried doing a different kind of book, it backfired. Superhero fans picked up a copy and then were annoyed because the book wasn't what they expected. Comic-book readers who didn't like superheroes never even noticed that this was a different sort of book.

The key, the publishers decided, was labeling. In the 1980s, DC created a new imprint called Vertigo. Vertigo books were still comic books and still published by DC, but they were a particular kind of comic book. Vertigo titles were darker, edgier, and more adult in their content. They had magic and heroes, but not people running around in capes and flashy costumes. One of the first Vertigo titles was a book by Neil Gaiman called *Sandman*, which focused on the master of dreams and his encounters with mortals and other supernatural beings. The book became a huge success, and Vertigo rapidly got several more titles. Now comic-book readers who wanted darker, more serious titles could look for Vertigo books, while fans of *Superman* and *Batman* could continue reading the regular DC line. Marvel tried doing the same thing but failed several times. It came close with the Marvel Knights books, which are about superheroes but have more adult themes and stories, and the Ultimate books, which are superhero comics but update the classic heroes so that new readers can identify with them more easily.

The question several fans asked was, why wasn't *Reign of the Zodiac* a Vertigo title? It was not a comic about superheroes, and it certainly didn't fit in with the

Neil Gaiman, seen here with Colleen Doran, is one of the most prolific writers working today. He is perhaps best known for writing the Sandman *series of comics, but he has since moved on to prose novels and screenplays. Gaiman has collaborated with Colleen Doran on more than one occasion. Doran provided the artwork for a chapter of his* Sandman *series, and Doran illustrated a story Gaiman wrote, "Troll Bridge," which is published in* A Distant Soil *number 25.*

rest of the DC universe. The more mature storyline and the more literary writing style would have fit more easily with Vertigo, and more readers might have noticed it. Perhaps DC felt that Giffen and Doran, who had both done superhero comics, were strong enough names that superhero fans would read their new book even though it didn't have any superheroes in it. If it had worked, DC could have shown its readers that not all DC comics had to be about superheroes. Instead, some readers who might have liked the comic book never saw it because it was listed as a regular DC book and not a Vertigo title, so they didn't realize that it was not a superhero book. And that confusion may have been why *Reign of the Zodiac* was canceled.

Of course, part of the problem was that the comic book was not easy to classify. It was not a superhero story, but it wasn't a standard Vertigo story either. Most Vertigo titles are set in the modern world and have some horror or magical elements. *Reign of the Zodiac* was set on another world, but one that felt like a fantasy setting. It was not dark enough to fit with the regular Vertigo books. That may have been what kept DC from putting it in that lineup. Giffen set out to write, and Doran to draw, a unique new story in a unique new world. And they did—but it may have been so unique that no one knew what to do with it.

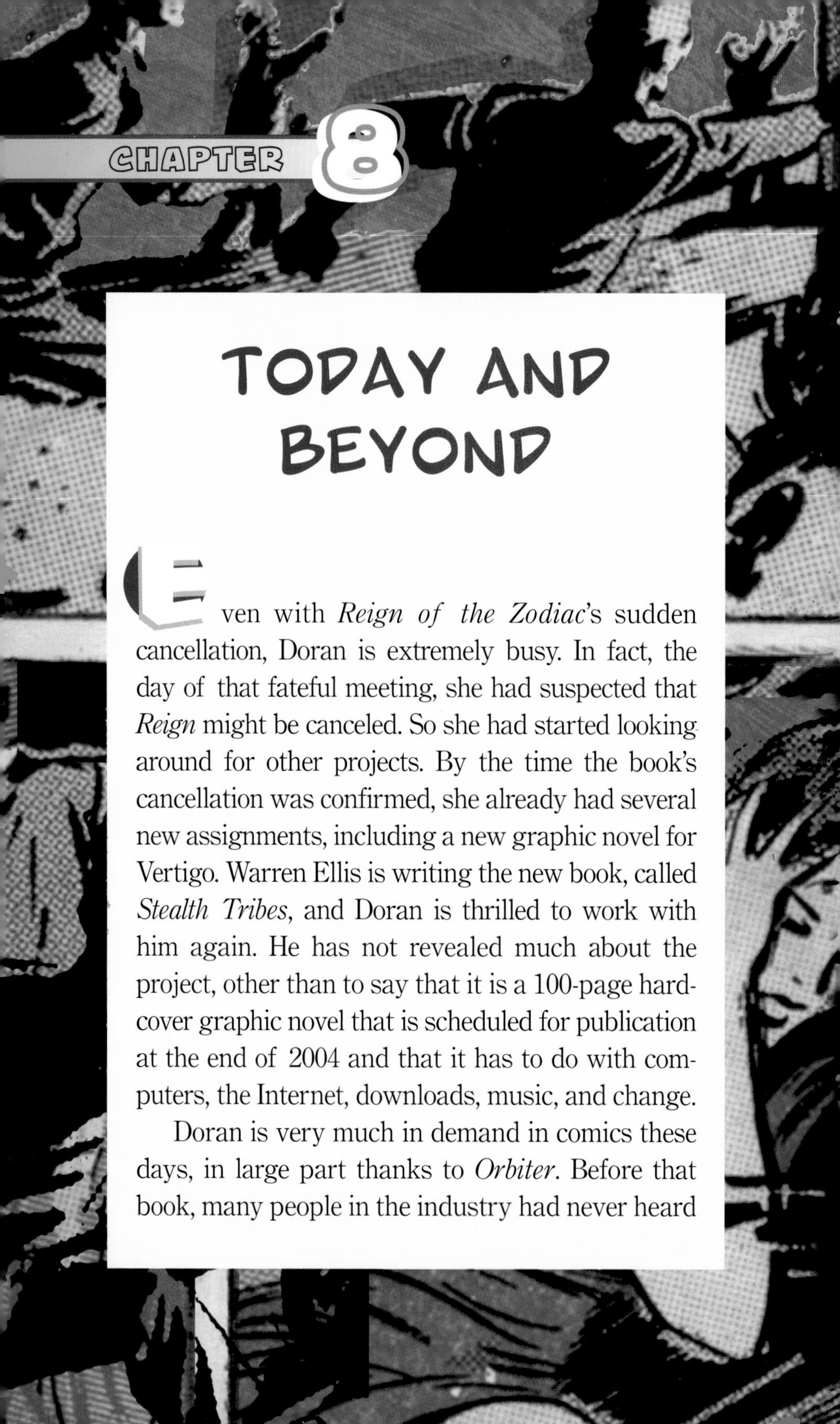

CHAPTER 8

TODAY AND BEYOND

Even with *Reign of the Zodiac*'s sudden cancellation, Doran is extremely busy. In fact, the day of that fateful meeting, she had suspected that *Reign* might be canceled. So she had started looking around for other projects. By the time the book's cancellation was confirmed, she already had several new assignments, including a new graphic novel for Vertigo. Warren Ellis is writing the new book, called *Stealth Tribes*, and Doran is thrilled to work with him again. He has not revealed much about the project, other than to say that it is a 100-page hardcover graphic novel that is scheduled for publication at the end of 2004 and that it has to do with computers, the Internet, downloads, music, and change.

Doran is very much in demand in comics these days, in large part thanks to *Orbiter*. Before that book, many people in the industry had never heard of her. Now everyone knows her name and respects her talent. Between *Orbiter* and *A Distant Soil*, Doran has demonstrated that she can draw in a variety of styles and do each one superbly.

She has recently finished another exciting project, this one outside the comic book industry. Doran got the opportunity to illustrate *The Essential J. R. R. Tolkien Sourcebook* by George Beahm. For someone as devoted to Tolkien's Middle-Earth series as Doran, this was a dream come true. The 259-page book contains detailed information about Tolkien's *The Lord of the Rings* trilogy (*The Fellowship of the Ring*, *The Two Towers*, and *The Return of the King*) and about Tolkien himself. It details Tolkien's correspondence, his manuscripts, and everything Tolkien-based from adaptations of his work to collectibles based on it to the Web sites created by the fans. The book was intended for people who had seen and enjoyed the movies and now wanted to find out more about the books the movies were based upon, and about the man who wrote them. Doran got to contribute several full-page black-and-white illustrations for the book and several smaller images as well. She particularly enjoyed the chance to draw some of the characters who wound up being left out of the movie, like Glorfindel and Elrond's two sons, Elrohir and Elladan.

Doran is also a member of the Society of Portrait Artists and occasionally creates portraits and other paintings as private commissions for people. She also does commissioned illustrations through her Web site, though only when she has time between other projects.

Here is one of several full-page illustrations Doran contributed to *The Essential J. R. R. Tolkien Sourcebook*. The book is for fans of Tolkien's series, especially those who became aware of the literature thanks to the popularity of the movies. Because of her work on the book, Colleen Doran was invited to the *Lord of the Rings: The Two Towers* Oscar party. Doran loves the series so much she is an official member of the *Lord of the Rings* fan club!

When she is not working, Doran likes to hike, jog, and garden. She has also done volunteer work, donating time over the years to the AIDS Housing and Education Fund, the Yorktown Shipwreck Archaeological Project, and the United Service Organizations (USO). She reads whenever she can, everything from Greco-Roman history to space science to pre-Raphaelite art texts to fiction (her favorite authors include Clive Barker, Harlan Ellison, Jane Austen, Dorothy Parker, and, of course, J. R. R. Tolkien). To offset her intellectual pursuits, she practices kick-boxing both for fun and for self-defense. Doran attends Renaissance fairs and often exhibits her work there. She even enjoys competitive rifle shooting.

Most of the time, though, Doran is busy drawing or painting. She has a lapboard in her bedroom and often works on illustrations late at night before falling asleep. Fortunately for her, she was able to hire a talented assistant several years ago, and it was someone Doran trusted completely—her mother. Her mother helps her handle business matters and finances, organizes her projects, helps run booths when they attend conventions, and even does some of the backgrounds on pages. Having the assistance lets Doran focus on the art itself and keep herself concentrated on the project at hand—or projects, since Doran likes to be working on several different things at once.

One thing Doran has mentioned in interviews and columns before is the need for organization, particularly in the form of time management. She is a habitual

THE CONTINUING STORY . . .

Doran has worked on *A Distant Soil* on and off for over half her life! Naturally, as she has grown, she has changed in many ways. But have these changes affected her work? In a 2003 interview for SlushFactory.com, Colleen discusses the evolution of *A Distant Soil:* "The basic plot hasn't changed one single bit. This may be stubborn or single-minded of me, but I am secure in my belief that the concept itself is solid enough to stand, even though I came up with it when I was twelve! However, the level of depth in the storytelling itself and in the characterization is a great deal more complex than originally conceived. The initial plot was for a superhero tale, but I dumped all the superhero trappings fairly early on, even though the story itself remained. I drew on a lot of my experiences as a young girl working as a professional artist from the age of fifteen and put a good deal of those anxieties and exploitative experiences into the story and characterization too. I have had many good reviews that remark on the psychological complexity of the work, and I would say that the writing I do now, as an adult, has a certain insight that I could not possibly have possessed as a twelve-year-old."

list-maker and always keeps two lists on hand: the list of projects she is working on and the list of non-work–related tasks she needs to do. Whenever she completes something on either list, she checks it off. Unfortunately, she rarely has the time to take care of the non-work list, but having it staring back at her every day keeps her from forgetting about those other chores and intended activities.

An Artist's Home

Though for many years she lived in a condo in Virginia, Doran finally got tired of the urban lifestyle. Her car was broken into more than once, her home was vandalized, and, in general, she watched as her neighborhood got dirtier and more dangerous. The last straw was when people broke into her car and removed components from her door, apparently because they needed the parts to repair their own vehicle and didn't feel like paying for them. Doran moved out.

She had been interested in buying an old barn and renovating it, but the costs involved ended up being more than she could easily afford. Also, the delay would have been far too long—she wanted out of the city as soon as possible.

Her family owned land and a home in rural Virginia, but Doran had gotten used to having her own space. Though she and her parents were close, she didn't want to move back in with them, so they compromised. She bought an old house and a nearby cottage on her parents' property and set about renovating them. For several months, Doran shuttled back and forth, moving belongings out of the apartment and into the house and then doing some work on the house before returning to the apartment, which she was also renovating so that she could sell it more easily.

The house is actually larger than she needs and had hideous wallpaper and wood paneling, but it has a beautiful garden and a nearby orchard. The cottage, which she transformed into her studio, had a chimney for a wood stove and excellent lighting, but little more than bare concrete on the walls. The biggest drawback to the move was the lack of Internet access, which made it harder for her to access her e-mail and update her bulletin board, and the lack of anything like a copy shop or a business supply store nearby.

But those difficulties were offset by the peacefulness of her surroundings. Simply being able to sit outside and draw without being disturbed was a wonderful opportunity, and Doran was thrilled with the chance to simplify her life and focus on her art and her family.

"Practical Matters"

Recently, Doran started an online column called "Practical Matters" at the Slush Factory Web site. Slush Factory is a site dedicated to pop culture and alternative comic books. In the first installment of her column, Doran warns that she is not going to talk about her favorite comics or anything like that. Instead, she offers extremely practical advice for would-be writers and artists. Thus far, she has talked about time management,

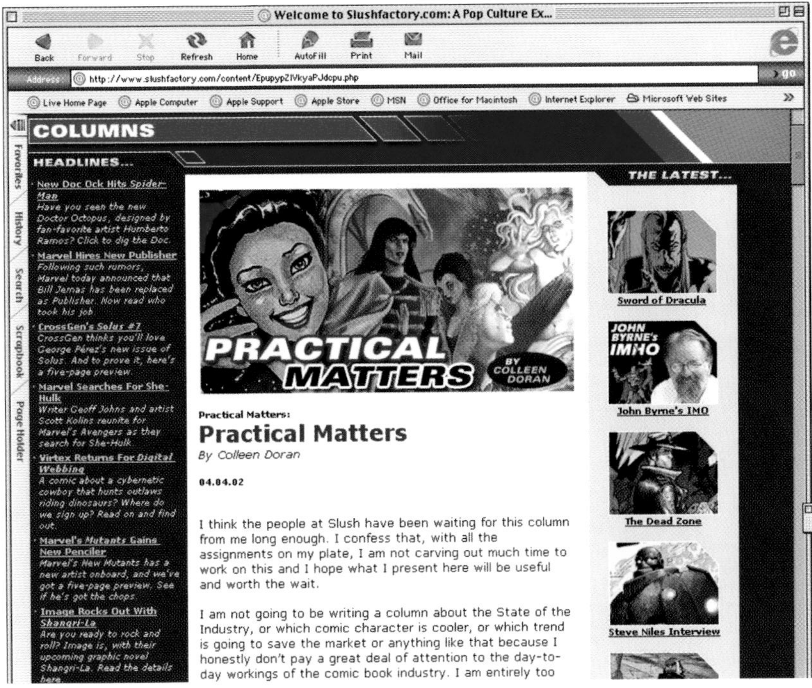

Colleen Doran contributes a column, "Practical Matters," to the Slush Factory Web site. A screen shot of her column is shown above. Although Doran admits she doesn't have much time to keep a regular column (there is often a year-long gap between entries), she gives realistic and useful advice to aspiring graphic novelists and those working in the industry.

handling money, and setting up an office in a way that ensures maximum workspace, comfort, and efficiency. She joked in one column about how writing an online column for free was low on her list of priorities, but the truth is many creators would not even bother to consider such a project.

Doran agreed to write the column because she likes helping people and because she feels that others can benefit from her years of experience. She also has a

VISUALIZATION

On her online bulletin board, Doran related a method she uses for overcoming creative blocks or artistic depression. Her happiest time as an artist was her childhood, when she drew and wrote simply because she loved it. Once she became a professional artist, business intruded and dulled that joy considerably. Stress, finances, and professional rivalries and other issues threatened to overwhelm her. Whenever Colleen feels overwhelmed by her art and by the pressures that accompany it, she takes a few minutes to sit and remember her youth and to re-create that environment in her head. She often does this by crawling back into her bed, playing music she used to listen to as a child, watching an old favorite film, and having milk and cookies or some other favorite childhood snack. Between visualizing her old life as a child and re-creating it as closely as possible, Doran found that she could revitalize herself by regaining that sense of wonder and joy art had brought to her as a child. She does mention on her board that this technique can take half an hour or more the first few times you try it, as you are learning how to visualize that setting again. But once you have more practice, you can conjure that scene and that feeling almost at will and use it whenever your creativity is overwhelmed by more mundane concerns. She also points out that athletes use a similar technique, visualizing their objective and recalling a comforting and nurturing environment so that they can perform their best during an athletic event.

bulletin board on her own Web site, and she frequently chats with people, offering suggestions, advice, and stories. One thing she will not do, however, is look at someone else's portfolio—mainly to protect herself. If someone sent her art samples, Doran would then be responsible for them, and that could cause all sorts of complications. By refusing to accept art samples from people and limiting her art critiques to online images, she protects herself from any responsibility. At the same time, that attitude helps beginning artists understand that art is a business and has to be handled that way. This is the same theme Doran has running through her columns, that this is a business, and it has to be approached practically and sensibly in order for the artist to succeed.

Another recent non-art project for Doran was her role in Rich Henn's *Scenes from the Small Press: Mainstream Raw* DVD and the follow-up piece, *Scenes from the Small Press: Colleen Doran*. Both are part of comic creator and filmmaker Henn's series of documentaries about the comic industry. In the *Mainstream Raw* documentary, he interviews Doran and several others, including Frank Miller and Matt Wagner. Henn's goal was to show what it was really like to work in the industry, both the good and the bad. The two-hour documentary has been hailed as entertaining, sobering, and enlightening. It is certainly a film that anyone who wants to work in comics should watch so that he or she can get a better idea what it is really like to work in that industry.

The second documentary is strictly about Doran herself. Henn interviews her extensively but also speaks to her mother to get a different perspective about Doran as an artist and a comic-book industry insider. He gets Doran to talk about several episodes from her past, including several unpleasant encounters with editors, publishers, and other industry figures. She talks about the darker periods of her life, when she almost gave up comics entirely, but also how she always managed to conquer the prejudices, bad breaks, and her own fears to get to the level she has reached today. It is an inspiring documentary about an immensely talented woman and demonstrates that you really can achieve your dreams if you work at them and never give up.

Doran has several valuable traits as an artist. She is obsessive about her work and extremely detail-oriented. She is also obsessive about cleaning and has joked that, if she couldn't be an artist, she could find work cleaning out her friends' houses. She often goes on cleaning binges, where she will spend a full day or more sorting through old files and dumping most of them. The advantage of this habit, she says, is that she often discovers belongings she had completely forgotten she owned, such as an original piece of art or a favorite book from childhood. She insists that each work be her best. She focuses upon character and nuance without losing action and setting. However, her greatest artistic gift is her versatility.

Many artists work to develop a distinctive style, which they use on everything. Doran is the opposite. She believes that the artist's job is to help tell the story

The DVD *Scenes from the Small Press* is a must-see for fans of Doran's work. The DVD shows Doran at work and relating her experiences in the comics industry. Her candor is refreshing, and her insights serve as practical advice for those whose goal is to make a living drawing comics.

ADVICE FROM COLLEEN

On the Web site for *A Distant Soil* (www.adistantsoil.com), Colleen Doran advises aspiring artists to simply practice to become better at what they do. It sounds simple, but as Doran says, many people say they want to be professional artists, yet they only draw about an hour a week! "If you're not drawing and/or writing in every spare moment, then you don't want it enough," Doran writes. "If you have time to watch TV, time to hang out at the mall, time to play video games, then you have time to practice your craft."

Doran also suggests reading all the books available about becoming a professional creator. The *Writer's Market* and the *Artist's Market* are both valuable guides to making a living at what you love most, if what you love most is creating art. Another idea is to attend conventions where creators are willing to give advice to their fans. If you can't make it to a convention, you can contact many professionals over the Internet.

and that the best way to do that is to find the style that suits that story best. When she works on *A Distant Soil*, she uses one style because that suits the story and the characters. But the same style would not work for *Orbiter*, so she had to develop a new style. *Reign of the Zodiac* required a third style, which did not match the other two. For each new project, Doran thinks about the project itself, the story, the characters, and the mood. She compares it to an actor getting ready for a role. Rather than concentrating on the way she draws, she thinks about what drawing style would best suit that particular assignment. She then does her best to lose herself in it, so the reader sees the story rather than seeing her. Some artists would complain if a reader did not recognize their work. Doran considers that a compliment because it means she has properly done her job by enhancing and conveying the story without being obtrusive. If the style she picked had not matched the story so well, it would have stood out, and that would have hindered the reader's enjoyment.

Doran's other gift is not about her talent but about her influence. She was one of the first women to self-publish, and she is the only woman with her own Image title. To most of the women in the industry, Doran is an image herself of strength and independence. She has weathered a variety of problems, from chauvinism to ageism to legal disputes. Doran has had her work blacklisted by publishers and almost stolen by others. She endured the industry crash when the distribution network collapsed and has seen several major projects disappear from under her. She has been told that women could not work in comics, that she had no talent, and that she could never draw for this project or that project. But she has survived all of that and is more popular and more sought-after than ever.

Doran is proof that women can make a living as comic-book creators. She speaks at conventions about the difficulties involved, but her goal is not to discourage

Although Doran laments that she and the other creators always come down with colds and respiratory illnesses after traveling to comics conventions, it is important to her to attend them and to touch base with her fans. Doran recognizes that her fans are responsible for her ability to continue making a living from comics.

people. Rather, she talks to educate them and to help them understand what they have to do. She goes out of her way to offer advice and support and to help others in the same way that people such as Keith Giffen and Frank Kelly Freas once helped her. No matter what else happens, she continues working. Ultimately, Colleen Doran loves what she does. She loves making art and telling stories, and she is one of the very best at it.

The End

SELECTED WORKS

Beahm, George. *The Essential J. R. R. Tolkien Sourcebook*. Franklin Lakes, NJ: New Page, 2004.

Doran, Colleen. *A Distant Soil: The Aria*. San Jose, CA: Image Comics, 2001.

Doran, Colleen. *A Distant Soil: The Ascendant*. San Jose, CA: Image Comics, 2000.

Doran, Colleen. *A Distant Soil: The Gathering*. San Jose, CA: Image Comics, 1999.

Doran, Colleen. *A Distant Soil: Knights of the Angel.* New York: Walsworth, 1989.

Ellis, Warren. *Orbiter*. New York: DC Comics, 2003.

Gaiman, Neil. *Sandman*: "Dream Country." DC/Vertigo graphic novel (collected series). New York: DC Comics, 1999.

Giffen, Keith. *Reign of the Zodiac*. New York: DC Comics, 2003–2004.

Hart, Chris. *Anime Mania: How to Draw Characters for Japanese Animation*. New York: Watson-Guptill, 2002.

Hart, Chris. *Manga Mania: How to Draw Japanese Comics*. New York: Watson-Guptill, 2003.

Reynolds, Kay, ed. *Robotech Art II*. New York: Walsworth, 1987.

Robbins, Trina. *Wonder Woman: The Once & Future Story*. New York: DC Comics, 1998.

Schlosser, James. *Anne Rice's The Master of Rampling Gate*. Wheeling, WV: Innovation Books, 1991.

SELECTED AWARDS

Delphi Institute Grant Award, 1989

Eisner Award Nominee, 1992, 1993

American Representative Japan/America Manga Seminar, Tokyo, 1996

Spectrum Award Nominee, 2000

Spectrum Award Finalist, 2001

American Library Association featured speaker, 2002

Chesley Award Nominee, 2002

San Diego Comic-Con guest of honor

Multiple awards and honors, various gallery exhibits

anime Japanese animation, comparable to American cartoons but usually with more detailed and stylized art and more complicated story lines.

coalesce To unite.

collect To reprint the issues of a comic book series together in a single volume.

comic book A book in which a story is told in sequential art, usually published in twenty- to thirty-page issues.

forensics The science of studying crimes, particularly evidence, in order to determine what happened and who was responsible.

genre A category of works that all have a similar theme, setting, or focus.

graphic novel A story told in sequential art and collected into a trade paperback.

inker The artist who goes over the penciler's work in ink, creating more details and shadows.

manga Japanese graphic stories that usually have very stylized art and are aimed at adult readers instead of children.

penciler The artist who draws the initial images for a comic book or graphic novel, usually in light pencils.

sequential art A series of images that form a story, like the frames of a film.

storyboard A panel or series of panels of images that depict the important changes of scene and action in a series of shots, as for a film, television show, or commercial.

FOR MORE INFORMATION

American Society of Portrait Artists
P.O. Box 230216
Montgomery, AL 36106
(800) 62-ASOPA (622-7672)
Web site: http://www.asopa.com

Association of Science Fiction and Fantasy Artists (ASFA)
P.O. Box 15131
Arlington, TX 76015-7311
Web site: http://www.asfa-art.org

Friends of Lulu
556 South Fair Oaks Avenue, Suite 48
Pasadena, CA 91105
Web site: http://www.friends-lulu.org

National Cartoonists Society
NCS Membership Committee
P.O. Box 713
Suffield, CT 06078
Web site: http://www.reuben.org

Web Sites

Due to the changing nature of Internet links, the Rosen Publishing Group, Inc., has developed an online list of Web sites related to the subject of this book. This site is updated regularly. Please use this link to access the list:

http://www.rosenlinks.com/lgn/codo

FOR FURTHER READING

Eisner, Will. *Comics and Sequential Art*. Tamarac, FL: Poorhouse Press, 1985.

Eisner, Will. *Graphic Storytelling and Visual Narrative*. Tamarac, FL: Poorhouse Press, 1996.

Hart, Christopher. *Drawing Cutting Edge Comics.* New York: Watson-Guptill, 2001.

Hogarth, Burne. *Dynamic Figure Drawing.* New York: Watson-Guptill, 1996.

Janson, Klaus. *The DC Comics Guide to Pencilling Comics.* New York: Watson-Guptill, 2002.

McCloud, Scott. *Understanding Comics*. New York: DC Comics, 1999.

Smith, Andy. *Drawing Dynamic Comics*. New York: Watson-Guptill, 2000.

BIBLIOGRAPHY

"Colleen Doran." Artbomb.net. Retrieved January 24, 2004 (http://www.artbomb.net/profile.jsp?idx=2&cid=3).

"Colleen Doran." Dragon*Con. Retrieved February 25, 2004 (http://www.dragoncon.org/people/doranc.html).

"Colleen Doran in Orbit and Amongst the Stars." Broken Frontier. Retrieved February 25, 2004 (http://www.brokenfrontier.com/snatch/2003/cdoranq&a.htm).

"Colleen Doran Interview." Westfield Comics. Retrieved December 21, 2003 (http://westfieldcomics.com/wow/frm_int_023.html).

Coville, Jamie. "Colleen Doran Interview." Coville's Clubhouse. Retrieved January 13, 2004 (http://www.collectortimes.com/2003_01/Clubhouse.html).

Handley, Derek. "A Discussion with Colleen Doran." Slush Factory. Retrieved December 18, 2003 (http://www.slushfactory.com/content/EpVuVuplAleqfgiDVl.php).

"Kelly Freas Biography." *Bud Plant Illustrated Books*. Retrieved February 19, 2004 (http://www.bpib.com/illustrat/freas.htm).

"The Legion of Super-Heroes Online Companion: Creators." *Legion of Super-Heroes*. Retrieved

January 3, 2004 (http://www.legiononline.net/volume5/creators.html).

Mason, Jeff. "Interview with Colleen Doran." Retrieved January 7, 2004 (http://www.indyworld.com/comics/doran.html).

The Official Website of Colleen Doran. Retrieved November 20, 2003 (http://www.colleendoran.com).

The Official Website of *A Distant Soil.* Retrieved December 2, 2003 (http://www.adistantsoil.com).

O'Shea, Tim. "Colleen Doran: Working Hard." SilverBulletComicbooks. Retrieved March 11, 2004 (http://www.silverbulletcomicbooks.com/features/106515332492810.htm).

Sebastian, Trisha Lynn. "Not So Distant Doran." *Sequential Tart*. Retrieved February 1, 2004 (http://www.sequentialtart.com/archive/feb02/doran.shtml).

WarrenEllis.com. Retrieved December 10, 2003 (http://www.warrenellis.com).

INDEX

About the Author

Aaron Rosenberg writes educational books, novels, and role-playing games, and he owns his own games company, Clockworks (http://www.clockworks.com). He grew up in New Orleans but now lives in New York.

Photo Credits

Cover photo, p. 95 © Martin Smith-Rodden; Cover (comics panels), title page, pp. 3, 14, 29, 32, 36, 39 © Colleen Doran. A Distant Soil is a registered trademark of Colleen Doran; p. 5 Maura B. McConnell; p. 7 Library of Congress Prints and Photographs Division; pp. 12, 82, 98 Courtesy of Colleen Doran; p. 13 X-MEN: ™ & © 2004 MARVEL CHARACTERS, Inc. Used with permission; p. 21 Cindy Reiman; p. 22 "Green Hills of Earth" © Frank Kelly Freas, 1977, 1984; p. 22 (photo) Courtesy of Laura Freas; p. 44 © AP/Wide World Photos; p. 47 Used with permission of Friends of Lulu (http://www.friends-lulu.org/); p. 48 Aquaman sketch Courtesy of Ramona Fradon; p. 48 (photo) Courtesy of Ramona Fradon, Charlie Roberts Photographer; p. 51 Greg Elms/Lonely Planet Images; p. 54 Frank Carter/Lonely Planet Images; p. 59 From MANGA MANIA: HOW TO DRAW JAPANESE COMICS by Christopher Hart. Copyright © 2001 by Christopher Hart. Reprinted with permission from the publisher, Watson-Guptill Publications, a division of VNU Business Media; p. 63 © Arnold Cedric/Corbis Sygma; p. 86 © Colleen Doran.

Many thanks to Colleen Doran for her assistance in providing imagery for this book.

Designer: Les Kanturek